Unlocking
Your
Destiny
Through the
Power of
Prayer

YOU WERE CREATED FOR GREATNESS
AND BORN TO MAKE AN IMPACT

Mwaka Twagirayesu

Copyright © 2007
Mwaka Twagirayesu
Fresh Aroma International Ministries
www.fresharomaministry.org

ISBN 978-1484945650

Printed in the United States of America

Editorial Services:
Jabez books Writers' Agency
(A Division of Clark's Consultant Group)
www.clarksconsultantgroup.com
972-424-2074

Unless otherwise indicated, scriptural quotations
are taken from the New King James Version of
the Bible.

Acknowledgements

To My Dearest Husband, Pastor and Mentor, Apostle Darius Twagirayesu. I attribute my spiritual growth and development to you. Thank you for seeing the gift in me and giving me countless opportunities to allow God to use me. I greatly value your friendship, mentorship, encouragement and apostolic counsel. Thank you for lecturing me about writing books. My first book has finally been birthed because of you! Many more books are on the way . . . It's such a joy serving the Lord together with you. I love and appreciate you.

Our Miracle boys, Zachary, Trey and Prince, you are the sunshine of my life. Your persistence in asking for "stuff" challenges my faith in God ! I love being your Mum.

My Mother, Ambassador, Dr. Inonge Mbikusita-Lewanika, "My modern day Proverbs 31 woman." Thank you for giving me a strong foundation in God. Your discipline and strictness paid off...look at me now! Your godly example and spirit of integrity and excellence continues to transform my life. I am honored to be your daughter.

My Late Father, Mr. Kabuka S.B. Nyirenda, "World's Best Dad." You were a brilliant scholar and distinguished statesman. You developed in me such a passion for reading and writing. Your generosity and kindness gave me a glimpse of what my Heavenly Father, ElShaddai, is like. You taught me how to love people from all walks of life. I miss you.

My sister, Nawina Matshona, your wisdom and prophetic insight never ceases to amaze me. You have always provoked me to go after God with all that is within me. Thank you for not letting me settle for second best and always reminding me of my uniqueness. You are a blessing.

My brother in law, Paul Matshona, thank you for your unwavering faith and confidence in me. All things are possible indeed!

My Spiritual Father, Archbishop Nicholas Duncan-Williams, I am grateful for your continual spiritual investment, impact and impartation in my life. Papa, your lifestyle of prayer and apostolic ministry has revolutionized my prayer life. You truly are The Chief Apostle of Strategic Spiritual Warfare. I appreciate you from the bottom of my heart.

My Spiritual Mother, Prophetess/Evangelist Teresia Wairimu, your life and ministry stirred in me such a passion for God and a hunger to operate in the supernatural. We will never forget how God used you to prophesy concerning our miracle boys, thank you for praying till they manifested! You are a treasure.

My Mentor, Prophet Bernard Blessing, thank you for activating the prophetic mantle upon my life. Your mentorship is priceless.

Dr. Shirley Clark and Jabez Books Staff Members - thank you for your wisdom, hard work and professionalism in editing, proofreading and publishing this book. You have been a tremendous blessing.

Our dear friends and co-laborers in ministry: Pastors Pacific and Salome Zagabe, thank you for consistency all these years. We treasure your covenant friendship. Pastors Eric and Nancy Matondo, thank you for your tremendous support and unconditional love; Pastor Peter Mccarn, thank you for the doors you opened; Pastor John and Joan Wachira for being an oasis, opening your hearts, home and ministry to us; Pastor and Mrs. Christopher Kamau for your wisdom; Bishop David Kalaya, thank you for the New England farewell. We will never forget your labor of love; Pastor Samuel Mutyaba, Ev. Suzette Ssajabbi, we remember the "All Nations" era in Boston with such fond memories...thank you for being a part of it all; Pastor Charles Karanja, you are precious friend. Bishop Esther Makumbi, we remember your message, "It shall come to pass!; Pastors Ben and Ivy Akotey, you are loved; Bishop Samuel and Jackie Kamuanga, keep the worship flowing; Apostle Jose and Pastor

Patricia Muzingu, you are appreciated; Pastor Ken Heath, thank you for your generous support of our Mission to Rwanda; and Apostle Brian Weeks, thank you for ministering to us in such a special way, Pastor Marilyn Weekes, Pastor Lorraine Thornhill, Pastors Sam and Marsha Wood, Rev. Robinah Katende, Pastor Mildred Lopes, Pastor Jared Mlongecha, Pastor Shupiwe Ngoma, Bishop Joshua Wambua, you all have been such a blessing.

Betty Ogaye, words cannot express my gratitude for your continued support, prayers, generosity, and willingness to serve. Thank you for your constant intercession and undergirding the vision God has placed within me.

Our Faithful Covenant Partners, thank you for your generosity – Katherine Nolan, Russel and Kecia Lopes, Catherine Kangethe, Susan Muriru, Susan Gicure, Rose Kimani, Catherine Wachira, Margaret Githinji, Gladys Kirika, Caroline Mbithi, Carol Mungai, Edwin & Peninah Idehen, Margaret Kingi, Jacinta Kangethe, Rev. Olivier Katanga, Shiko Ndungu. Ev. Priscilla Mushi, Ev. Freda Sebalu, Rev. Margaret Masuwa, Jane Ndlovu, George Kizito, Thomas Kinyanjui, Theresa Chirwa, Sarah Saroni, Josephine and Quincy Fellowship, you are a very special group of brethren; Dan Kamau -- Jamhuri Magazine; and Kimani Karanja -- Kenya Live TV, you play an instrumental role. Thank you for your media coverage.

My co workers at United Homes For Children, Inc., Tewskbury, Massachusetts – Ed Malone, Denise Washington, Susan O'Connor, Ronald Frost, Evelyn Vadea and Karen Chapas. I learned so much during my 10 years with you all, what a great team of professionals you are. By the way, how are you managing without me?

The Body of Christ in Massachusetts and New England region, it has been a joy to live, love and serve Jesus together with you. God used our 17 years in New England to train, shape, mold, and prepare us for a glorious destiny. You play a significant role in our lives. We are divinely connected for life.

Thank you very much for receiving us in our new place of assignment. The Lord bless and make His face shine upon you all.
Betty Ogaye, Pastor Jean Marie, Eddy and Rachel Niragira, Valentine and Janvier Busogi, Elizabeth Oduor, Dennis and Damaris Kimani, Fred and Grace Chege, Eric and Musi, Paul and Anne Lamptey, Julius and Charity Mwangi, Stephen Kamau, Mumbi and Chege, Jesse Maringa, Emmanuel Ogiozee, Kelechi Eke, Pastor Valentine and Edith Egbudiwe, Ev. Hilda Kahia, Pastor William Bittock, Pastors Philip and Rebecca Mwonga, Pastor Uzo and Winnie Agulefo , Pastor Kim and Wade Vastine, Pastors Robert and Susan Jima, Pastors Jackson and Lucy Kingori, Pastor and Mrs. John Muturi, Pastor Thomas and Jane Kariuki.

Dedication

This book is dedicated to those in the Body of Christ who are dissatisfied with the status quo, a mediocre and stagnant life and realize that our God is ElShaddai and has so much more for us than what we are experiencing now and that He desires to pour out His Spirit in an unprecedented measure through the power of prayer.

Contents

Introduction

This book was birthed out of my great and overwhelming desire to see "The Book of Acts" become a reality in my life. I was studying and meditating on the tremendous impact that the early church made in their community and nation through the power of prayer and this ignited an overwhelming spiritual hunger in my life.

After 17 years of pastoring, church planting, and pioneering ministries in New England, the Lord sent our family to Dallas, Texas in July 2007. July is the seventh month. Seven is a prophetic number signifying, *Rest, Perfection, and Completion.*

The Lord has been revealing to His Servants and His people throughout the year of 2007 that this is a prophetic year for the Body of Christ. It is a year of **Manifestation** and **Fulfillment**. He will complete everything that concerns us. He will demonstrate His Power. In the midst of calamity and tragedy in the world, the Lord will preserve His people for the advancement of His Kingdom and to reveal His glory upon the earth, through His praying people.

We begun to seek the Lord earnestly about His Prophetic Purpose for our lives. We begun to ask God why He brought us to Dallas, and we knew it was more than just to live in a nice house and drive a nice car. The Lord is a God of purpose and design. I knew we hadn't driven thousands of miles from New England to Dallas for nothing! God had something on His mind for us! God had a mighty work for us in Dallas, Texas!

In our first few weeks of being in Dallas, everywhere we went, we met ministers and believers who were in some type of transition. They were hungering for more of His presence in their lives, and many were dissatisfied with their current jobs, positions and status in life, and locations. However, they all had an understanding that there was a spiritual shift taking place. This was a confirmation to us that our relocation from New England had a huge prophetic significance and we had a Prophetic Purpose and Destiny to fulfill.

I became so thirsty for the presence of the Living God and so desperate for the Lord to manifest Himself and reveal His Purpose, Plan and Prophetic calling in my life. It was so intense that I began to cry out in prayer so desperately for a fresh infilling of the Holy Spirit, for His fresh impartation -- fresh oil, fresh anointing, fresh fire, and fresh revelation.

Jeremiah 29:13 declares, *"...And you will seek me and find me when you search for me with all your heat."* As I began to earnestly and sincerely seek the Lord, He began to reveal Himself and His purpose and plan for my life. The Lord began to speak to me in those precious moments of seeking Him.

I challenge you, my beloved brothers and sisters in the Body of Christ, let us come out of mediocrity, defeat and complacency; and take our rightful positions as God's covenant people in the earth. Let us shake off spiritual slumber, spiritual laziness, spiritual procrastination, and the spirits of doubt and unbelief. It is time to **"Arise, shine for your light has come and the glory of the Lord is risen upon you"** (Isaiah 60:1).

Through our prayers, millions will come into the Kingdom of God. Through our prayers, cities and nations will be transformed by the glory of God. Through our prayers, economies and governments will be touched by the power of God. Through our prayers, we will unlock our destinies and fulfill our prophetic purpose on the earth.

With all the calamities, catastrophes, tragedies, earthquakes, floods, plane crashes that we see in the news, the Church of Jesus Christ needs to arise in prayer like never before. This is the season to pray. **Isaiah 55:6-7 says, *"Seek the Lord, while He may be found, Call upon Him while He is near, Let the wicked forsake His way, and the unrighteous man his thoughts, Let him return to the Lord, and He will have mercy on Him and to our God, For He will abundantly pardon."***

We are co-laborers with God through prayer. What an honor to partner with God through prayer to see His purposes established on the earth. God moves upon the earth when we pray. He intervenes supernaturally in the affairs of man when we pray. *He looked for a man to stand in the gap and found none* **(Ezekiel 22:30).**

Abraham is not only known as the Father of Faith and a friend of God, he was also an intercessor. His example of prayer shows how one committed person's prayer can make a difference. He stood in the gap for the wicked cities of Sodom and Gomorrah and because of his intercession, his nephew Lot was spared. *"And Abraham came near and said, Would you also destroy the righteous with the wicked? Suppose there were fifty righteous within the city, would you also destroy the place and not spare it for the fifty righteous that were in it? Far be it from you to do such a thing as this, to slay the righteous with the wicked, so that the righteous should be as the wicked, far be it from you! Shall not The Judge of all the earth do right" (Genesis 18:23-25).*

Abraham kept negotiating with God in prayer. He told the Lord, You cannot destroy both the righteous and wicked, together. He reasoned with God in prayer! He told God to spare the righteous, if he could find fifty righteous. He was persistent in his intercession. Eventually, he asked God to spare the righteous, even if it was just ten righteous individuals. What would have happened if Abraham had not interceded? Lot would have been destroyed with the rest of Sodom and Gomorrah. What happens when we as believers do not intercede? The enemy causes havoc, calamity, accidents, tragedies, etc. Remember his mission according to **John 10:10** is to steal, kill and destroy.

Your prayers are very significant. Your prayers make a difference. When two people pray in one accord, the results are even greater. *"How could one can chase a thousand, and two put ten thousand to flight"* (**Deuteronomy 32:30**)? God has given us so much power and authority as believers and when we come in agreement and in one accord joining our faith, power and authority, the enemy has no choice but to flee. *"Again I say to you, if two of you agree on earth concerning anything they ask, it will be done for them by my father in heaven. For where two or three are gathered in my name, I am there in the midst of thee"* (**Matthew 18:19-20**). There is tremendous power when we come in agreement on any matter in the name of Jesus. Our Heavenly Father will answer our prayers.

God wants to hear from you. Your voice is a mighty weapon in His hands. There is no distance in prayer. He has promised in **Isaiah 65:24**, *"It shall come to*

pass, that before they call, I will answer, and while they are yet speaking I will hear." What an amazing scripture. Before we even pour out our hearts, our God will answer us and while we are speaking to Him in prayer, He hears us! I pray that you will purpose in your heart to be a man or woman of prayer.

My prayer is that this will not just be another book on prayer for you to add to your library, but the passion to pray will be ignited in you by the Holy Spirit!

Chapter 1

Dissatisfaction of the Status Quo

We are living in a generation that is flooded by information. We are blessed to have numerous Christian television stations, thousands of Christian bookstores, and thousands of Christian conferences around the world. Through the media (television, radio, internet, mp3's, ipod's, and many other forms of technology) and various versions of the Bible, plus concordances and biblical dictionaries, we have all of these to help us in our understanding of the Word of God. All over the world, there are powerful churches and ministries that are preaching and teaching the Word of God. Bibles

Colleges, Seminaries and Theology Schools can be found in almost every nation and city, each teaching future Ministers the Word of God. Therefore, we, in the Body of Christ cannot say, we have not heard the Word of God. We have access to more than enough Christian material and information to equip and empower us for victorious living.

Despite the abundance of Christian information and material, there is still a cry in the earth for more than what we are presently experiencing. **Romans 8:19 says, *"For the earnest expectation of the creation eagerly waits for the revealing of the sons of God."*** In other words, even the world despite its sophisticated technology, high rise buildings, unlimited wealth, and abundant resources, etc is still crying out for the spiritual and supernatural. They have a void that money, position or status cannot satisfy. This void in their hearts can only be filled by Jesus Christ, Son of the Living God. Many in the world are turning to psychics and astrologers for answers and direction, but where are the people of God? Where are God's powerful people who are supposed to be full of the Holy Spirit and flowing in the gifts of the Spirit? The world should be turning to us for answers and solutions. It's time that we, the Body of Christ, arise in power and cause astrologers, psychics, palm readers, fortune tellers and witches, and those who operate with familiar spirits, to go out of business.

Where is the power of God in the House of God today? Why is it that only a few operate and flow in the gifts of the Spirit? In **Mark 11:15,** Jesus with holy anger, overturned the tables in the temple because it had become "A House of Merchandising" instead of "A House of Prayer." Through prayer, we release the anointing of the Holy Spirit to break yokes off peoples' lives, to set the captives free and deliver those that are bound. It is prayer that sets the atmosphere in the House of God, so that when sinners and backsliders enter into the House of God, they are convicted by the presence of the Holy Spirit.

What the world needs to see is not eloquent preaching and articulate speaking, but they need to be first hand witnesses of the power and glory of God! This is not to say, we should not present the Gospel clearly and articulately, or be organized and systematic in our presentation, but without the anointing and power of God in our messages, it's of little effect. An example of this is Apostle Paul. The Apostle Paul was a highly educated attorney and had studied for many years to become a Pharisee of the highest order. He was a distinguished scholar, academician and fluent in Hebrew and Greek. Yet, when he gave his life to the Lord, he underwent a complete metamorphosis. He said in **1 Corinthians 2:1-5,** *"And I brethren when I came to you, I did not come with excellence of speech or of wisdom declaring to you the* *testimony of God. For I determined not to know anything among you except Jesus Christ and him crucified, I was with you in weakness, in fear, and in much trembling. And my speech and my preaching were not with persuasive words of human wisdom, but in demonstration of the Spirit and of power, that your faith should not be in the wisdom of men but in the power of God."*

Personally, I am dissatisfied with the present day status quo. Yes, conferences are great, church programs have a role to play, but when conferences are not transforming lives for His glory, then what is the point of having them? When church services and programs are nothing but routines, procedures and man-made traditions, and worse still, people leave church worse than when they came, then we in the Body of Christ need to do something about our current lukewarm state of affairs. **We need to pray for His presence and glory to be in our midst!**

What made the early church, the church in the book of Acts, such a phenomenal church? **It was a praying church**. Prayer was the key to their success and impact. In **Acts 1**, one hundred and twenty people were praying earnestly and sincerely, while seeking the Lord and waiting for the infilling of the Holy Spirit. These days of waiting upon the Lord revolutionized their lives, and all who came in contact with them!

The joy of the Lord in them was infectious, their love for Christ was contagious and the power of God at work in their lives was evident for all to see. Their secret is found in **Acts 2:42-47,** *"And they continued steadfastly in the apostles' doctrine and fellowship in the breaking of bread and in prayers. Then fear came upon every soul, and many wonders and signs were done through the apostles. Now all who believed were together and had all things in common and sold their possessions and goods and divided them among all, as anyone had need. So continuing daily with one accord in the temple and breaking bread from house to house, they ate their food with gladness and simplicity of heart, praising God and having favor with all the people. And the Lord added to the church daily those who were being saved."*

It never ceases to amaze me how the early church did not have a television ministry or radio program. They had no sophisticated computer technology or church software to promote them. But they learned how to tap into the supernatural power of God through prayer! They were consistent, constant and dedicated to prayer and the Word of God. As a result, there was an explosion of miracles, breakthroughs, signs and wonders that caused the community to take notice. Prayer made their hearts tender towards God and one another so that no one in their midst was in need! Now that's what I call power! May that day come in the Body of Christ when there will not be such a large gap between the haves and have not's. May that day come in the Body of Christ when those who have more than enough, share willingly and joyfully with those who do not have enough. Prayer brought supernatural unity and harmony in the early church as well as hunger for the presence of God and the Word of God. They could not get enough of the Word of God! They enjoyed fellowship with one another; they had thankful hearts and a spirit of gratitude. It was God who gave them favor with people to the extent that *"The Lord added to the church daily, those who were being saved" (Acts 2:47).* With all due respect to present day marketing strategies, evangelism, community outreach plans, but church growth comes from the Lord!

The early church understood the power of prayer. They made prayer their priority. They were powerful because they prayed. People even recognized that they were servants of God. *"Now when they saw the boldness of Peter and John and perceived that they were uneducated and untrained men, they marveled" (Acts 4:13).* They ministered powerfully because they prayed. *"And when they had prayed, the place where they were assembled together was shaken and they were all filled with The Holy Spirit, and they spoke the word of God with boldness" (Acts 4:31).*

Their prayers brought such transformation to the community that the religious and political leaders of that day took note, but some were incensed. King Herod imprisoned Peter, the apostle, but God delivered him because of the consistent prayer of the saints. *"Peter was therefore kept in prison, but constant prayer was offered to God for him by the church. Now behold an angel of the Lord stood by him and a light shone in the prison and he struck Peter on the side and raised him up saying, Arise quickly and his chains fell of his hand. And when Peter had come to himself, he said, Now I know for certain that the Lord has sent his angel and has delivered me from the hand of Herod and from all the expectation of the Jewish people" (Acts 12:5,7,11).*

The apostles were persecuted for preaching the Gospel, but they were not deterred. They were determined to continue for the cause of Jesus Christ. Paul and Silas after a great move of God were imprisoned. They could have had a pity party, spent the night complaining and murmuring about their condition. Despite their challenge, they lifted up their voices to God in prayer and praise. *"But at midnight, Paul and Silas were praying and singing hymns to God and the prisoners were listening to them. Suddenly there was a great earthquake, so that the foundations of the prison were shaken and immediately all the doors were opened and everyone's chains were loosed" (Acts 16:25-26).*

The Prophet Joel sounded a clarion call to the nation of Israel. The Lord, our God is calling His people in this generation back to prayer in this season. *"Blow the trumpet in Zion, consecrate a fast, call a sacred assembly, gather the people, sanctify the congregation, assemble the elders, gather the children and nursing babes, let the bridegroom go out from his chamber, and the bride from her dressing room. Let the priests who minister to the Lord, weep between the porch and the altar. Let them say spare your people, O Lord and do not give your heritage to reproach that the nations should rule over them" (Joel 2:15-17).*

Notice that this was a clarion call to all, not just a few members of society, but to all: the. priests, elders, men, women, children and newlyweds! Many times we have relegated prayer to "intercessors", but every believer is commanded to pray. I **Thessalonians 5:17** declares, *"Pray without ceasing."* **Luke 18:1** says, *"Men ought always to pray and not lose heart (faint).* Here the word, "men" is referring to mankind.

If you are tired of the "same old, same old", so instead of complaining, do something about it! Pray! If you are sick and tired of being sick and tired! Pray! **James 5:13 says, *"Is anyone among you suffering?***

Let him pray." If your marriage is in shambles, arise in prayer! If your business is deteriorating instead of flourishing, pray! Pastor or evangelist, if your church or ministry is not growing and making an impact, you need to pray like never before. Jesus was our example. Even though He was the Son of the Most High God, He prayed. ***"And when He had sent the multitudes away, He went up on the mountain by Himself to pray" (Matthew 14:23).*** After powerful healings and deliverances to multitudes, Jesus prayed. After a great move of God, He still prayed. ***"Now in the morning, having risen a long while before daylight, He went out and departed to a solitary place and there he prayed" (Mark 1:35).*** So many people with all manner of sicknesses, infirmities, diseases and afflictions were following Jesus and His disciples to receive from Him, and because of this, he would always withdraw to a quiet place to pray and receive refueling from His Father. "

The Word of God says Elijah, the Prophet, had weaknesses, shortcomings, failures like any human being, yet, he was a powerful prayer warrior. He prayed that there would be no rain for three and a half years, and it did not rain. Then, he prayed again, and it rained! **Here's how it was recorded in the New Testament in the book of James 5:16-18, *"The effective fervent prayer of a righteous man avails much. Elijah was a man with a nature like ours and he prayed earnestly that it would not*** *rain, and it did not rain on the land for three years and six months. And he prayed again, and the heaven gave rain, and the earth produced its fruit."* The word "**effective**" in Merriam-Webster's Dictionary means the power to bring about a result, to cause to happen, producing a desired outcome or an intended effect, exerting positive influence, to be fruitful. In other words, when we pray, we should experience the results of our prayers. We are also to be **righteous** before God, in right standing with our God. Our hearts should be free from sin, guilt and condemnation. If we have fallen short, we can ask for forgiveness, *"If we confess our sins, He is faithful and just to forgive us our sins and to cleanse us from all righteousness" (1 John 1:9).*

Our Heavenly Father loves to answer the prayers of His people. He is no respector of persons. If we can follow the principles of the Word of God, we will experience breakthroughs and miracles. If we honor Him and are obedient to His Word, He will gladly hear and answer our prayers. *"Then Peter opened his mouth and said in truth I perceive that God shows no partiality. But in every nation whoever fears Him and works righteousness is accepted by Him" (Acts 10:34).*

We are exhorted in **Romans 12:12** to *"continue steadfastly in prayer."* Many make the mistake of only praying when they are in trouble or facing challenges. However, as believers, we have a command and a mandate to pray daily and continually, even in the good times, we need to pray. *The key is to stop talking, reading and discussing prayer, and actually pray!* Regardless of your age, gender, ethnicity, socioeconomic status, education level, you can touch the heart of God through prayer. God is not a respector of persons.

The question is who is willing to stand in the gap? Who is willing to position themselves for God to use in the ministry of intercession? Who is willing to sacrifice their time and pleasure to avail themselves in prayer that the strongholds of the enemy may be aborted so that the purposes and will of God may be established? May it not be said of our generation that God was looking for a vessel He could use in the ministry of prayer, supplication and intercession, but found no one willing to pay this price. *"Then The Lord saw it, and it displeased Him, that there was no justice, He saw that there was no man, and wondered that there was no intercessor"* **(Isaiah 59:15-16).**

Beloved, **prayer changes everything.** It is true that there is a tremendous price to pay. It is true that it will involve your time, energy, and you forfeiting pleasures of sleep and food. It is true that it is not always easy to respond to the voice of the Holy Spirit, when He wakes you at 3:00 a.m. to pray (just when sleep is the sweetest)! But, oh, it is so worth it in the end! Jesus endured the pain and shame of the cross for the glory and honor that awaited Him.

Let's get sick and tired of being sick and tired! Our Lord Jesus Christ is **NOT** coming back for a church that is broke, bust and disgusted. He is **NOT** coming back for a weak, defeated, and pathetic church. He is coming back for a glorious and triumphant people. The church is the Bride of Christ. Our Bridegroom is coming back for a bride that is clean, pure, without spot and blemish. Just like a bride glows, sparkles and is radiant on her wedding day, so should we, the spiritual Bride, be glowing and radiant with the power and presence of God, which can only comes through extended time in His presence. It is the anointing of the Holy Spirit that destroys the yoke. The anointing is released when we pray. *"It shall come to pass in that day, that his burden will be taken away from your shoulder, and his yoke from off your neck, and the yoke will be destroyed because of the anointing"* **(Isaiah 10:27).**

We, as God's people, have a mandate to pray not only for ourselves, but for our families, neighborhoods, communities and nations. *"If my people who are called by My Name, will humble themselves and pray and seek My face and turn from their wicked ways, then I will hear from heaven and will forgive their sin and heal their land"* **(2 Chronicles 7:14).** The Lord promises to hear from heaven and heal our land as we turn to Him in humility and repentance.

Chapter 2

We have been given access

Jesus paid a tremendous price through His death on the cross of Calvary for you and me to have access to the throne of grace. When Jesus died one of the things that happened immediately was that the curtain that hid the Holy of Holies in the tabernacle was torn apart. The Holy of Holies was reserved for the priests in times past. Only a select group of priests had access to the Holy of Holies. The curtain being torn apart was significant in that it symbolized that all could have access to the Father regardless of age, gender, ethnicity, socio-economic status or education. If you are born again and Jesus

Christ is the Lord and Savior of your life, you have access!

Ephesians 2:13-14 states, *"But now in Christ Jesus you who once were far off have been brought near by the blood of Christ. For He Himself is our peace, who has made both one, and has broken down the middle wall of separation."* Once we were far from God because our sin had separated us from Him. However, through the blood that was shed on Calvary, through His Son Jesus Christ, we have the covenant right to come near, praise God! Ephesians 3:12 says, *"...In whom we have boldness and access with confidence through faith in Him."* In fact, we are admonished to come near to God, to come to His throne of grace with boldness and confidence.

As a child of God, the Word of God urges you to come boldly to the throne of grace. *"Let us therefore come boldly to the throne of grace, that we may obtain mercy and find grace to help in time of need"* (Hebrews 4:12). You do not have to be afraid; God's throne is a throne of grace, mercy and compassion. Whatever you need, you will find it at His throne. In His presence you will find wisdom for decision-making, instruction for your life, revelation for your mind, victory for your life, joy and peace for your heart and so much more.

You can approach the throne of grace boldly and confidently because according to

Ephesians 2:19, "...*You are no longer strangers and foreigners, but fellow citizens with the saints and members of the household of God.* Only strangers and foreigners are intimidated and fearful! You are a member of the household of God and a citizen of the Kingdom of God, so you have every right to speak to your Heavenly Father in prayer and get the results of your prayer!

The Lord is not only our God, He is our Father! **Romans 8:15,** *"For you did not receive the spirit of bondage again to fear, but you received the Spirit of adoption by whom we cry out Abba Father. The Spirit Himself bears witness with our spirit that we are children of God and if children, then heirs-heirs of God and joint heirs with Christ, if indeed we suffer with Him, that we may also be glorified together."*

Not only do we have access to our Heavenly Father and not only are we His covenant children, but we are according to **Ephesians 1:6b,** *"accepted in the beloved."* No wonder John, The Beloved declared in **1 John 3:1,** *"Behold what manner of love the Father has bestowed on us, that we should be called the children of God."*

You do not need to be a Greek or Hebrew scholar to pray. You do not need a degree in Theology to get your prayers answered! Remember, God is a loving Heavenly Father who loves to hear from His

31

children in prayer and enjoys answering them. **Matthew 7:7 says, *"Ask and it will be given to you, seek and you will find, knock and it will be opened to you. For everyone who asks receives, and he who seeks finds and to him who knocks it will be opened. Or what man is there among you if his son asks for bread, will give him a stone? or if he asks for a fish will give him a serpent? If you then being evil know how to give good gifts to your children, how much more will your Father who is in heaven give good things to those who ask Him."***

As natural parents, we will go out of our way to ensure that our children, not only have the basic necessities of life such as food, clothing and education, but we will go above and beyond providing the basic neccessities to indulge them with toys, vacations, gifts, and extra curricular activities to demonstrate our love. As humans, our love is so temporal, limited and conditional. Now imagine our loving Heavenly Father whose love is immeasurable, unlimited, permanent and unconditional! Our Heavenly Father loves to answer the prayers of His children.

God, our Heavenly Father, gave the world His very best. He gave us His Son, Jesus Christ. He could have chosen one of the angels (archangels, seraphims or cherubims) to come to the earth to die for our sins, but instead, He chose the very best heaven had - *"He who did not spare His own Son, but delivered Him up for us all, how shall He not with Him freely give us all things" (Romans 8:32).* Surely if Abba Father could give us His very best, His Son, Jesus Christ, He is willing to give us our hearts' desires.

My friend, there are so many scriptures concerning our Father's desire to answer our prayers! *"Now this is the confidence that we have in Him, that if we ask anything according to His will, He hears us. And if we know that He hears us whatever we ask, we know that we have the petitions that we have asked of Him" (1 John 5:14-15).* This scripture alone is enough to give you such joy and assurance that your Heavenly Father is just waiting to hear your petition, and will gladly and willingly answer you!

Jesus taught a lot on prayer. He told His disciples in **Matthew 6:5-8,** *"And when you pray, you shall not be like the hypocrites, for they love to pray standing in the synagogues and on the corners of the streets, that they may be seen by men. Assuredly I say to you, they have their reward. But you when you pray, go into your room, and when you have shut your door, pray to your Father who is in the secret place and your Father who sees in secret will reward you openly. And when you pray do not use vain repetitions as the heathen do. For they think they will be*

***heard for their many words.* "** It is not the amount of words we use in prayer or the type of advanced vocabulary that impress God! He is impressed by our simplicity, sincerity and trust in Him.

We are exhorted to pray to our Father in the Name of His Son, Jesus, ***"And in that day you will ask Me nothing. Most assuredly, I say to you, whatever you ask the Father in My Name he will give you. Until now you have asked nothing in My Name. Ask and you will receive, that your joy might be full" (John 16:23-24).*** There is nothing as pleasurable as answered prayer! There is nothing as refreshing as laboring in prayer and then enjoying the rewards or fruits of your labor in prayer.

Do not be afraid to ask. ***"You do not have because you do not ask" (James 4:2).*** Even though our Heavenly Father knows our needs and desires, He wants us to ask. Just like children are so bold in asking their parents to meet their needs when they are hungry, thirsty and want to go somewhere, etc, we, too, need to ask unashamedly. Do not limit or restrict God in your asking. Many times we only ask for small things as though God will fall off the throne if we make a big request! The Dow Jones, Stock Market and NASDAQ are all affected by inflation, but the economy of heaven is intact, in shape and still going strong. We, as believers, should not be moved by a fluctuating economy. If you are a faithful tither in the House of God and a generous giver in the kingdom of God, our Heavenly Father will take care of you.

The access we have been given to the throne of grace is not just to pray for our own needs, but to pray for others. We, as believers, have a responsibility to pray for our nations, governments and leaders. We need to pray for our Presidents, Senators, Congressmen or Congresswomen, and the entire judiciary system.

Every person in authority, need our prayers. We need to pray that the Lord may not only save them, but fill them with His Spirit that they may rule and reign in wisdom. It is crucial that we have a prayer covering over our leaders, so that ungodly legislation may be abolished, and in its place, rules and regulations that promote godliness, equality truth and justice prevail. *"Therefore I exhort first of all that supplications, prayers, intercessions, and giving of thanks be made for all men, for kings and all who are in authority, that we may lead a quiet and peaceable life in all godliness and reverence" (1 Timothy 2:1-2).*

Chapter 3

The Power of the Holy Spirit

As Jesus was nearing the completion of His assignment on the earth, **Acts 1:4** declares, *"And being assembled together with them, He commanded them not to depart from Jerusalem, but to wait for the Promise of the Father, which He said, you have heard from Me for John truly baptized with water, but you shall be baptized with the Holy Spirit not many days from now.* Jesus told His disciples to wait for the infilling of the Holy Spirit because He knew the Holy Spirit would transform their lives for effective ministry. *"But you shall receive power after the Holy Ghost is* *come upon you and you shall be witnesses to Me in Jerusalem and in all Judea and Samaria, and to the end of the earth" (Acts 1:8).* Each of us is called to be a witness starting in our homes, workplaces, neighborhoods, communities and nations. It is through the power of the Holy Spirit that we become effective witnesses.

In obedience to the instruction from Jesus, *"These all continued with one accord in prayer and supplication, with the women and Mary the mother of Jesus and with His brothers" (Acts 1:14).* Initially, there were 500 disciples who waited upon the Lord in prayer and supplication. Then, the number was reduced to 120 disciples. Our flesh is never eager to pray and wait upon the Lord. The enemy will bring so many distractions when it is time to pray...you suddenly feel sleepy, tired, hungry, bored, etc. The remnant who crucified their flesh and tarried in the upper room, waiting for the outpouring of the Holy Spirit were touched by the power of God in a phenomenal way.

The outpouring of the Holy Spirit brought such a major transformation in their lives that it was evident to the community that the disciples had been changed! Peter, who in the past seemed somewhat unstable and hot tempered, and even denied being a disciple of Jesus, now became a powerful Apostle who ministered with such power, authority and boldness all because he took time to wait on the Lord in prayer. *"Now when they saw the boldness of Peter and John and perceived that they were uneducated and untrained men, they marveled. And they realized they had been with Jesus. And seeing the man who had been healed standing with them, they could say nothing against it" (Acts 4:13).*

The Holy Spirit not only empowers us for service, but He teaches us how to pray while interceding through us, when we yield to Him and are sensitive to His presence and leading. **Romans 8:26-27 says, "Likewise the Spirit also helps in us our weaknesses. For we do not what we should pray for as we ought, but the Spirit himself makes intercession for us with groanings which cannot be uttered. Now He who searches the hearts knows what the mind of the Spirit is, because He makes intercession for the saints according to the will of God."**

The beauty of allowing the Holy Spirit to pray through us is He prays according to the Will of God. Sometimes the English language seems so limited in expressing our desires to God. If you are going through a crisis or dilemma and cannot express your pain or anguish in words, let the Holy Spirit pray through you. You may be overwhelmed by personal challenges and feeling spiritually weary, let the Holy Spirit pray through you.

The Holy Spirit is our companion, teacher, counselor, friend and helper. He helps us in prayer. **John 16:7-8 states it this way, "Nevertheless I tell you the truth. It is to your advantage that I go away, for if I do not go away, the Helper will not come to you, but if I depart, I will send Him to you. And when He has come, He will convict the world of sin and of righteousness, and of judgment."** Let us make room for the Holy Spirit to move in and through us. It is the Holy Spirit that brings conviction. As we sacrifice in prayer and become doers of the Word, and not hearers only, the Holy Spirit will convict backsliders around us and those living a double life.

If we want to pray effectively, we must position ourselves to receive the power of the Holy Spirit. What a difference the Holy Spirit makes! He anoints, equips and empowers us to pray. Prayer should never be a drag. It should never be boring, dull or monotonous. We must allow the Holy Spirit to pray through us and in us. The Apostle Paul said in **1 Corinthians 4:20, "The Kingdom of God is not in word, but in power."**

The world must see the demonstration of the power of God through us. That power is released in us when we pray. The early church operated in the supernatural power of God because they were a praying church. The sick were healed, demons were cast out, and the bound were set free. What was the result? The church kept growing, increasing and multiplying. Why, because of the power of prayer! *"And believers were increasingly added to the Lord, multitudes of both men and women so that they brought the sick out into the streets and laid them on beds and couches that at least the shadow of Peter passing by might fall on some of them. Also a multitude gathered from the surrounding cities to Jerusalem, bringing sick people and those who were tormented by unclean* spirits *and they were all healed" (Acts 5:14-16).*

The apostles in the early church operated in an extraordinary anointing because they were praying men. Miracles were the order of the day. When Dorcas, also known as Tabitha, died there was great weeping in Joppa, as she had been a blessing to so many. They summoned for Peter, the Apostle, *"But Peter put them all out and knelt down and prayed. And turning to the body he said, Tabitha arise. And she opened her eyes, and when she saw Peter she sat up. Then he gave her his hand and lifted her up, and when he had called the saints and widows, he presented her alive. And it became known throughout all Joppa, and many believed on the Lord"* (Acts 9:40, 42).

When you have done all you know to do - prayed, fasted, and stood on the Word - allow the Holy Spirit to take over because it is *"Not by might or by power, but by Spirit says the Lord"* *(Zechariah 4:6b).*

Sometimes we try in our own flesh to solve problems. We try to reason naturally and attempt in our own strength to solve problems. There are some matters that are so severe and complex it takes the supernatural intervention of God. When we pray, we are giving room for the Holy Spirit to intervene on our behalf.

Sometimes it seems the enemy has so much more power. It seems that he is advancing and gaining ground, but praise God, our God is far greater, far mightier and more than able! *"When the enemy comes in, like a flood the Spirit of the Lord will lift up a standard against him." (Isaiah 59:19).*

As we eat food daily to keep our bodies healthy and nourished, we need a daily dose of the Word of God and prayer. We build and strengthen our inner man through prayer. We must make time to pray, in fact, the busier we are, the more we need to make a conscious effort to pray. If we can make time to watch our favorite programs on television, return telephone calls, respond to emails, chat with friends on the telephone, etc., then surely we can find the time to pray! Sometimes it will require taking the telephone off the hook, respond to the email later, and postpone the trip to the mall to get in the presence of the Living God! *"But you beloved, building yourselves up on your most holy faith, praying in The Holy Spirit" (Jude 1:20).*

As believers, we need to remain in that constant communion, fellowship and intimacy with our Heavenly Father. As natural parents look forward to daily communication with his or her child, so our Heavenly Father looks forward to our companionship and relationship with Him in prayer. He wants to hear from us not only when we are in crisis or in danger, but even in the good times. Prayer is not a one time event. It is not a weekly, biweekly or monthly event! It is not enough to attend Friday prayer meeting at church or an annual prayer conference! Each of us must have a prayer life. It is great to have prayer partners and prayer teams, but it is imperative that you have your own personal time of prayer with the Lord. The Word of God exhorts us in the following manner, *"Praying always with all prayer and supplication in the spirit" (Ephesians 6:18a).*

With all the catastrophes, calamities and tragedies we witness daily in the news, we, the Church of Jesus Christ, need to crucify our flesh and pray like never before. It is time to allow our inner man to take over. In the garden of Gethsemane, Jesus told the disciples, *"Could you not watch with me one hour. Watch and pray, lest you enter into temptation. The spirit is indeed willing, but the flesh is weak" (Matthew 26:41).*

Chapter 4

Praying the Word

Jesus defeated Satan in the wilderness through the Word of God. Jesus did not argue or negotiate with Satan, He simply stated, *"It is written, man shall not live by bread alone, but by every word that proceeds from the mouth of God" (Matthew 4:4).*

The enemy fears the Word of God because he knows that God and His Word are one. God cannot violate His Word. He means what He says and He says what He means. God and His Word are inseparable. *"In the beginning was the Word and the Word was with God and the Word was God" (John 1:1).*

It is imperative for you, Child of God, to know the Word of God and to know that the promises of God are for you. When you come to that revelation that the Word of God is not just a story book, but it is the infallible, unchanging Word of the Living God, your prayer life will change. As you approach God in prayer, you pray with confidence, knowing in your spirit that God fulfills His Word. ***"He watches over His Word to perform it" (Jeremiah 1:12).***

The Word of the Lord is so powerful. In the beginning when the entire earth was dark and void, God spoke His Word and brought forth life through the spoken word. We know that our Lord and Savior, Jesus Christ has been given a name that is above every name. The name of Jesus is far higher and greater than the power of principalities, powers and spiritual wickedness in high places. Yet, the Word of God declares in **Psalms 138:2b,** *"You have exalted your word above all your Name."* The Word of God is supreme. The Word of God is sovereign. The Word of God is eternal. *"Heaven and earth will pass away, but My Word will by no means pass away" (Matthew 24:35).*

Our God is a promise keeper and a Covenant keeper. If He has promised you that you will go to school to advance your studies, then you will. If He has promised that you will be a successful business man or woman, then you will. You have to know the Word of God for yourself and go to Him in prayer and remind Him of a scripture in His Word that fits your situation. **Psalms 89:34 states, *"My Covenant I will not break, nor alter the word that has gone out of my lips."***

God promises His people that His Word shall not return void. In other words, what the Lord has spoken concerning your life, it will not and cannot return back empty. The Word of the Lord concerning you shall come to pass. The Word of the Lord shall be fulfilled. ***"For as the rain comes down and the snow from heaven, and do not return there, and water the earth, and make it bring forth and bud, that it may give seed to the sower and bread to the eater, so shall my word be that goes forth from My mouth, it shall not return to me void. But it shall accomplish what I please and it shall prosper in the thing for which I sent it" (Isaiah 55:10-11).***

The key to answered prayer is abiding in His presence and allowing the Word of God to abide in us. We have to transform our thinking, mentality and perspective with the Word of God. We must believe His Word and let it sink deep into our spirits. ***"If you abide in Me and My words abide in you, you will ask what you desire, and it shall be done for you"* (John 15:7).**

The Word of God is our blueprint for success. The Word of God reveals who we are in Christ. We are children of the Most High God, sons and daughters of the King of Kings! *"But you are a chosen generation, a royal priesthood, a holy nation, His own special people that you may proclaim the praises of Him who called you out of darkness into His marvelous light, who once were not a people, but are now the people of God, who had not obtained mercy but now have obtained mercy"* *(1 Peter 2:9-10).*

In addition, **Revelations 1:6a** says, *"...And has made us kings and priests"* **unto our God.** Knowing who we are in Christ, we can pray boldly, confidently and with great expectancy. We must refuse to be denied! We must refuse the packages of the enemy. The packages of the enemy are sorrow, poverty, misery, depression, sickness, confusion, etc. According to **John 10:10,** *Jesus came to give us life and life more abundantly!*

This is not to say we will not go through challenges, storms and tribulations, but we can go to God in prayer, *"Many are the afflictions of the righteous, but the Lord delivers us from them all"* **(Psalms 34:19).** The enemy will try his best to frustrate and hinder us. He will try to show us that God does not answer prayer and that the Word of God is not working, but we must persevere in prayer like the widow in the parable Jesus told His disciples about. Even though she was dealing with a wicked judge, she was persistent until she got her request! *"...There was in a certain city a judge who did not fear God nor regard man. Now there was a widow in that city and she came to him saying, Get justice for me from my adversary. And he would not for a while, but afterward he said within himself, though I do not fear God nor regard man, yet because this widow troubles me I will avenge her, lest by her continual coming she weary me. Then the Lord said, Hear what the unjust judge said, And shall God not avenge His own elect who cry out day and night to Him, though he bears long with them" (Luke 18:2-7).*

Chapter 5

Weapons of Our Warfare

Jesus is not coming back for a weak, defeated, broke and busted church!! He is coming for a glorious and triumphant people. We really have no excuse in not getting results in prayer because we are made in the image and likeness of the Almighty God. We should not be weaklings in prayer because we have been equipped and armed with weapons. Just like in a natural army, soldiers have weapons (machine guns, ammunition, etc.), so likewise we, as soldiers of the Most High God, have been given spiritual weapons of mass destruction!

In **Genesis 1:26-28, God said,** *"Let us make man in our image, according to*

Our likeness, let them have dominion over the fish of the sea, over the birds of the air, and over the cattle, over all the earth and over every creeping thing that creeps on the earth. So God created man in His own image, in the image of God he created him, male and female He created them. Then God blessed them, and said to them, Be fruitful and multiply, fill the earth and subdue it, have dominion over the fish of the sea, over the birds of the air and over every living thing that moves on the earth."

The word **"image"** according to Merriam-Webster's Dictionary means, "a likeness or imitation of a person or thing, a person strikingly like another person, a carbon copy, a representation of another" The word **"likeness"** means, "a pictorial representation of a person, one that resembles or corresponds to another, the quality or state of being like. **"Dominion"** means, "supreme authority, to rule." **"Subdue"** means, to conquer and bring into subjection, to bring under control, to conquer and overpower.

Right from the beginning of creation, when we were being created, God had a plan for His children to walk in dominion and authority. Child of God, we did not come from apes! We were created in the image and likeness of the Almighty God. In other words, we have God's power flowing through us or supreme authority over the schemes of the enemy. The enemy has come to steal, kill and destroy according to **John 10:10.** He tries to steal from God's children through inflicting disease in their bodies, depression in their minds, poverty in their finances, conflict and strife in their families, etc.

We are commanded in the Word of God to take dominion through prayer over every hardship, affliction or misfortune the enemy tries to throw our away. We must exercise our God-given authority over every obstacle, hindrance, barrier, resistance and delay of the enemy through prayer. We do not pray as beggars or wimps, but we pray with authority and power knowing that we are *more than conquerors*, according to **Romans 8:37.** As we pray, we bring into subjection every demonic spirit that tries to prevail against us. As we pray through the power of the Holy Spirit, we conquer and defeat the purposes and plans of the enemy and establish the purpose of God. *"You have made him to have dominion over the works of your hands, you have put all things under his feet"* (**Psalms 8:6**).

When we pray, we pray from a position of victory because **Ephesians 2:6** says *"...And raised us up together, and made us sit together in the heavenly places in Christ Jesus."* In other words, we are seated in heavenly places with Christ Jesus, far above all principalities and powers. Your voice is a mighty weapon in the heavenlies! Your prayer knows no distance.

You can be in one location and great deliverance takes place in another location because of your prayers.

Your prayer is like having an account with God. Just like you deposit money into a bank account, when it comes to withdrawal, you are able to withdraw because of the deposits you have made. Your prayers are a memorial before God. *"There was a certain man in Caesarea called Cornelius, a centurion, a devout man and one who feared God with all his household who gave alms generously to the people and prayed to God always. About the ninth hour of the day, he saw clearly in a vision, an angel of God coming in and saying to him, Cornelius! And when he observed him, he was afraid, and said, what is it Lord, the angel said, Your prayers and your alms have come up for a memorial before God" (Acts 10:1-4).*

To enter a specific door, you need specific keys. Not every key will unlock your front door; you have a specific key for your front door, side door, back door, etc. We, too, have supernatural keys to open specific doors in the supernatural. *"And I will give you the keys of the Kingdom of heaven and whatever you bind on earth, will be bound in heaven, and whatever you loose on earth will be loosed in heaven" (Matthew 16:19).*

51

God has given us powerful weapons of warfare that we can use in prayer to defeat the purposes, evil schemes and tricks of Satan. **2 Corinthians 10:3-4 states,** *"For though we walk in the flesh, we do not war according to the flesh. For the weapons of our warfare are not carnal, but are mighty in God for pulling strongholds, casting down arguments and every high thing that exalts itself against the knowledge of God, bringing every thought into captivity to the obedience of Christ."*

What are these strongholds Apostle Paul is talking about? Sickness and infirmity, depression and fear, violence and anger, bitterness and resentment, divorce and unforgiveness, pride and arrogance, alcoholism and drug addiction, perversion and pornography, there are all sort of bondages and oppressions that the enemy has released upon the Body of Christ. Anything that you battled with for a very long time becomes a stronghold. Individuals have strongholds, families have strongholds, cities and communities have strongholds, nations have strongholds. This explains why some families are plagued by divorce, while others have longstanding healthy marriages; some cities are enterprising, while other communities are stagnant; some nations are prosperous, while others are overtaken by poverty.

We cannot combat these strongholds with our natural abilities. We need supernatural weapons of warfare to destroy these strongholds once and for all. Jesus told His disciples that a "strong man" (evil spirit) needs to be bound -- *"Or how can one enter a strong man's house and plunder his goods, unless he first binds the strong man and then he will plunder his house"* *(Matthew 12:29).*

Inside the Word of God, we find numerous weapons to fight with:

The Name of Jesus
We approach our Heavenly Father in the Name of Jesus Christ. His Name is above every name on the face of this earth. His Name is above every disease and infirmity. His Name causes Satan and his demons to scatter and flee. *"Therefore God also has highly exalted Him and given Him the name which is above every name, that at the Name of Jesus every knee should bow, of those in heaven and of those in earth, and of those under the earth, and that every tongue should confess that Jesus Christ is Lord to the glory of God the Father" (Philippians 2:9-11).*

The Lord Jesus Christ resides in each of us who have accepted Him as Lord and Savior of our lives. When we pray, we are not praying in our own strength or ability *"because He who is in you is greater than he who is in the world" (1 John 4:4b).*

Not only have we been given the powerful, glorious and majestic name of Jesus, we can also use the names of God. He is **Jehovah Nissi** which means **"Our Banner of Victory"**. He is **Jehovah ElGibbor**, which means **"A Man of War"**. He is **Jehovah Sabbaoth**, which means **"Lord of Hosts"**. He is **Jehovah El-Elyon**, which means, **"The Most High God"**. He is **Jehovah Mangenenu** meaning, **"The Lord, Our Defender"**. *"You are my King, O God, Command victories for Jacob, through you we will push down our enemies, through your Name we will trample those who rise up against us" (Psalms 44:4-5)*.

People put their trust in so many things. Some put their trust in their status in society; others put their trust in their high powered connections. Some put their trust in their mutual funds and investments; others put their trust in their education and scholastic achievements and awards. We, as children of the Most High God, know who to put our trust in .The name of the Lord, Our God! *"Some trust in horses, some trust in chariots, but we will remember the name of the Lord Our God" (Psalms 20:7)*.

Whatever you may be facing today, do not be afraid. The Lord is your refuge, defense, fortress and hiding place. *"The Name of the Lord is a strong tower, the righteous run to it and are safe" (Proverbs 18:10)*.

The Word of God

We defeat the enemy with the Infallible, Immutable Word of God. *"In the beginning was the Word and the Word was with God and the Word was God. And the Word became flesh and dwelt among us and we beheld His glory, the glory as of the only begotten of the father, full of grace and truth" (John 1:1, 14).* The Word of God has creative power. As we declare the Word of God in prayer, we destroy the strongholds of the enemy and establish the will and purpose of God. *"For The Word of God is living and powerful and sharper than any two edged sword, piercing even to the division of soul and spirit, and of joints and marrow, and is a discerner, of the thoughts and intents of the heart" (Hebrews 4:12).*

The Blood of Jesus

The blood of Jesus that was shed on Calvary two thousand years ago, not only cleanses us from sin and protects us from evil, it also gives us access to enter the Holy of Holies to enable us to have an audience with God. *"Therefore brethren, having boldness to enter the Holiest by the blood of Jesus" (Hebrews 10:19).* We overcome the enemy by the blood of Jesus, *"And they overcame him by the blood of the lamb and by the word of their testimony" (Revelations 12:11).*

Fasting

As we crucify our flesh, abstain from food and cry out to God in prayer and fasting, strongholds are destroyed and the power of God will invade our lives. *"Is this not the fast that I have chosen, to loose the bonds of wickedness, to undo the heavy burdens, to let the oppressed go free and that you break every yoke" (Isaiah 58:6)?*

Faith

Faith is one of the greatest weapons against the enemy. No matter what he tries to do, we remain steadfast and unmovable, trusting in the Lord, our God to make a way where there seems to be no way. Against all odds, we continue to stand on the Word of God and declare His promises concerning us. Faith means being unmoved by the natural circumstances. Our spiritual father, Abraham, believed God for a miracle baby. Even though he was 100 years old and his wife was 90 years old, he did not consider their old age, but trusted that God who gave the promise would execute and fulfill it. *"And not being weak in faith, he did not consider his own body already dead, since he was about a hundred years old, and the deadness of Sarah's womb, He did not waver at the promise of God through unbelief, but was strengthened in faith, giving glory to God and being fully convinced that what He had promised, He was also able to perform." (Romans 4:19-21).*

Obedience

Obedience is the key to walking under an open heaven. Obedience is the key to answered prayer. We can pray and fast for 40 days, but if we are disobedient to the voice of God and disobedient to His Word, our prayers are in vain and we will not receive anything from the Lord. *"And whatever we ask, we receive from Him, because we keep His commandments and do those things that are pleasing in His sight" (1 John 3:22).*

Are you tired of struggling? Are you tired of living your life bound by a cycle of defeat and failure? Has your entire life been afflicted by setbacks, hardships, calamities, tragedies and misfortunes? Check to see if you have been obedient to God's voice lately. Have you followed His instructions? *"If you are willing and obedient, you shall eat the good of the land, but if you refuse and rebel, you shall be devoured by the sword" (Isaiah 1:19-20).*

Our relationships are extremely significant to God. You might be wondering what our relationships have to do with answered prayer! The way we relate and treat people is of utmost importance in the eyes of God. We cannot claim to be prayer warriors or intercessors, and treat God's people harshly, disrespectfully or with cruelty. This is not to say we are to open our hearts to every person who comes our way. Obviously, we have to be selective. However, we have a responsibility to see people through the eyes of God and treat them with respect and love. *"And you shall love the Lord your God with all your heart, with all your soul, with all your mind and with all your strength. This is the first commandment, and the second, like it, is this, you shall love your neighbor as yourself" (Mark 12:30-31).*

Our relationships with our spouses are of utmost importance to God. We cannot pray heaven down and then treat our spouses with insensitivity and disrespect. In fact, the more we are in His presence and in His Word; the more the fruit of the Spirit is birthed in us. Remember, the relationship between a husband and a wife is symbolic of the relationship between our Lord and Savior, Jesus Christ and we, His bride, the Church. We, therefore, have an obligation and are commanded to walk in love, compassion, mercy, patience and forgiveness towards our spouses -- *"Husbands, likewise dwell with them with understanding, giving honor to the wife, as to the weaker vessel, and as being heirs together of the grace of life, that your prayers may not be hindered" (1 Peter 3:7).* The Word of God exhorts husbands to understand their wives, deal with them graciously, patiently and respectfully so that your prayers can reach heaven!

"Wives submit to your own husbands, as to the Lord, For the husband is head of the wife, as also Christ is head of the Church and He is the Savior of the body. Husbands love your wives just as Christ also loved the Church and gave himself for her, that he might sanctify and cleanse her with the washing of water by the Word" (Ephesians 5:22-23, 25-26).

In this scripture, wives are commanded to submit to their husbands as unto the Lord. Submission is not weakness; it is yielding to another's authority. Submission becomes a joy and a pleasure when it is done in a spirit of love and humility. The issue of submission has been misunderstood. Some have misinterpreted the word 'submission' and have used it to oppress, abuse and demean their wives. Submission should be done willingly and honorably as unto the Lord, and not by coercion. In my own life, submission to my husband became a joy when I understood the revelation that as I submitted to my husband, I was submitting to the Lord. Husbands are given the greater responsibility of loving their wives **"as Christ loved the Church and gave Himself up for her."** This is an unconditional sacrificial love; it means a commitment to love even when you don't feel like it. , It means considering your spouse before yourself.

Let us repent of any disobedience, sin, compromise, stubbornness and unteachable spirits in our own lives. If not, these spirits will hinder the work of the Holy Spirit in our lives and gives the enemy the upper hand. When we confess our sins, the Lord will cleanse us and make us whole. *"Behold The Lord's hand is not shortened, that it cannot save, nor his ear heavy, that it cannot hear, but your iniquities have separated you from your God, and your sins have hidden his face from you, so that he will not hear" (Isaiah 59:1-2).* When we fall short, thank God we have a Heavenly Father who is ever merciful and gracious, willingly to forgive and restore us, when we sincerely repent. His promise is that He will cleanse us and forgive us our sin.

Thanksgiving

Thanksgiving and praise is a powerful weapon! King Jehosophat understood this principle and defeated a host of armies that came out against him! *"And when he had consulted with the people, he appointed those who should sing to the Lord, and who should praise the beauty of holiness, as they went out before the army and were saying, Praise the Lord, For His mercy endures forever. Now when they began to sing and to praise, the Lord set ambushes against the people of Ammon, Moab and Mount Seir who had come against Judah and they were defeated. For the people of*

Ammon and Moab stood up against the inhabitants of Mount Seir to utterly kill and destroy them. And when they had made an end of the inhabitants of Seir, they helped to destroy one another" *(2 Chronicles 20:21-23).*

The whole atmosphere was changed as Israel began to sing praises unto the Lord. Their enemies became confused and turned on each other instead! When we praise God in the midst of turmoil, the enemy gets confused because he expects to find us overwhelmed and despondent, but instead finds us exalting our God. As we praise, the Lord intervenes. *"But you are holy, enthroned in the praises of Israel"* *(Psalms 22:3).*

As you pray, give thanks to God that He has heard you and will answer you. Pray with a spirit of gratitude and thanksgiving knowing your Heavenly Father delights to answer your prayer. *"Be anxious for nothing, but in everything by prayer and supplication, with thanksgiving, let your requests be made known to God and the peace of God which surpasses all understanding will guard your hearts and minds through Christ Jesus." (Philippians 4:6).*

The Apostle Paul exhorted the church in Ephesus in **Ephesians 6:10-17,** *"Finally my brethren, be strong in the Lord and in the power of His might. Put on the whole* *armor of God, that you may be able to stand against the wiles of the devil. For we do not wrestle against flesh and blood, but against principalities, powers, against the rulers of the darkness of this age, against spiritual hosts of wickedness in the heavenly places. Therefore take up the whole armor of God, that you may be able to withstand in the evil day, and having done all, to stand. Stand therefore, having girded your waist with truth, having put on the breastplate of righteousness, and having shod your feet with the preparation of the gospel of peace, above all, taking the shield of faith with which you will be able to quench all the fiery darts of the wicked one. And take the helmet of salvation and the sword of the Spirit which is the Word of God."*

Our strength is not in our education, gifts, talents, skills, abilities, work experience, ministerial accomplishments, societal status, or political connections. Our strength is in our God; that's why the Psalmist David said, "*I will look to the hills from whence cometh my help, my help comes from The Lord, who made heaven and earth" (Psalms 121:1).*

The Word of God exhorts us to put on the whole armor of God. The armor of God consists of the following:

➢ **Helmet of Salvation**

You must be born again. *"Unless one is born again, He cannot see the Kingdom of God"* (**John 3:3**). You must know Jesus as your personal Lord and Savior. *"If you confess with your mouth the Lord Jesus and believe in your heart that God has raised Him from the dead, you will be saved"* (**Romans 10:9**). He must live in your heart. You cannot stand against spiritual wickedness in high places in your own power. You need the power of Jesus in you.

➢ **Breastplate of Righteousness**

To be effective prayer warriors, we must ensure that our lives are clean and pure in the sight of God. If we have sinned in any way, we must repent and ask for His blood to cleanse us from all sin, unrighteousness and wickedness. *1 John 1:9 says, "If we confess our sins, He is faithful and just to forgive us our sins and to cleanse us from all unrighteousness."* Unconfessed sin, the root of bitterness and unforgiveness in our hearts becomes a stronghold of the enemy. *"Be ye holy as I am holy" (1 Peter 1:15).*

➤ **Belt of truth**

Jesus said, *"I am the way, the truth and the life, no one comes to the Father except through me" (John 14:6).* As we live submitted and yielded lives to the Holy Spirit, the more we will walk with Him; we must do away with falsehood and lies. Jesus said in **John 8:32,** *"And you shall know the truth, (which is His Word) and the truth will make you free."* His Word and His Spirit transform us to be people of truth and integrity.

➤ **Shield of Faith**

As you pray, pray in faith believing the Lord is a mighty Man of War. Have faith that He will deliver you. He will heal you. He will provide for you. He will make a way for you. You can go on a 40 day fast, but if you do not have faith, your fasting is in vain. As you fast, pray in faith that chains of bondage and oppression are being broken off your life. Pray in faith that ancestral yokes and generational curses are broken off your life. Pray in faith that the spirit of poverty is being broken off your life. And pray in faith that the spirit of strife and discord is being broken in your marriage, family and home. *"Therefore I say to you, whatever things you ask when you pray, believe that you receive them, and you will have them" (Mark 11:24).*

➤ Sword of The Spirit

The Sword of the Spirit is the Word of God. To prevail over the enemy, we must know the Word. Study the Word of God. Meditate on the Word of God and be doers of the Word. *"This Book of The Law shall not depart from your mouth, but you shall meditate on it day and night, that you may observe to do according to all that is written in it, for then you will make your way prosperous, and then you will have good success" (Joshua 1:8).*

Using all these weapons - the Name, the Blood, the Word of God, and the Whole Armor of God - will enable us to be strategic, effective and victorious in warfare. The schemes and tricks of the enemy will be exposed. His plans will be scattered. His strongholds will be destroyed and the kingdom of darkness will be defeated.

Our prayers are so powerful; they are likened to incense in the nostrils of our Heavenly Father. *"Now when He had taken the scroll, the four living creatures and the twenty four elders fell down before the Lamb, each having a harp, and golden bowls full of incense which are the prayers of the saints"* (Revelations 5:8b).

Chapter 6

The Prayer of Faith

Prayer is not about the number of elaborate words we use. Prayer is also not about our eloquent speech. Prayer is a heartfelt conversation with God. **Hebrews 11: 6 says,** *"But without faith it is impossible to please Him, for he who comes to God must believe that He is, and that He is a rewarder of those who diligently seek Him."* The Word of God is very clear. When we approach God in prayer, we must believe that He hears us and that He desires to answer us. We must believe that no matter how complicated the matter is, He can make a way, where there seems to be no way. We must believe that the time we are spending in His presence asking, seeking and knocking is not in vain and that *"He is a rewarder of those who diligently seek Him."*

The pioneer of the Word of Faith Movement, the late Kenneth Hagin, revolutionized the Body of Christ with his outstanding teachings on faith. His favorite scripture was, Mark **11:22-24**, *"So Jesus answered and said to them, "Have faith in God. For assuredly, I say to you, whoever says to this mountain, Be removed and be cast into the sea and does not doubt in his heart, but believes that those things He says will be done, he will have whatever he says. Therefore I say to you, whatever things you ask when you pray, believe that you receive them and you will have them."*

No matter what the circumstances look like, have faith in God. In other words, believe that He is well able to bring you out. Believe that as you pray, mountains are being leveled and God is moving on your behalf. Your language after prayer determines your victory. It is amazing how many believers after a powerful prayer meeting will speak negatively about their condition. If you have faith, even before the answer manifests, your language should be positive like you already have the answer! The scriptures declare, *"He will have whatever he says."*

Our language must change after we have prayed the prayer of faith. In other words, as we await the answer, we must speak positive faith-filled words. *"And since we have the same spirit of faith, according to what is written, I believed and therefore I spoke, we also believe and therefore speak" (2 Corinthians 4:13.)* After we have prayed, our conduct and actions must demonstrate we have faith. *"Thus also faith by itself, if it does not have works is dead" (James 2:17).*

As we pray, we are also admonished to forgive. It is not a choice, it is a command! As we forgive those who have offended, hurt or wounded us, whether intentionally or unintentionally, our Heavenly Father will also forgives us for our sins, weaknesses, shortcomings, temptations, etc. *"And whenever you stand praying, if you have anything against anyone, forgive him, that your Father in heaven may also forgive you, your trespasses. But if you do not forgive, neither will your Father in heaven forgive your trespasses"* (Mark 11:25-26).

Our hearts must be clean and pure before the Lord. When we are sensitive to His Spirit, He will show us our hearts and whether we are harboring any bitterness, anger or unforgiveness towards someone. Therefore, to get results in prayer, we have to forgive.

The Word of God is clear that when we approach God in prayer, we have to approach Him in faith. If we want to see results in prayer, we must believe that our

God can make impossible matters possible, hard situations easy. He is a giant slaying, mountain moving, barrier breaking God! All power and dominion belong to our God. He is omnipotent and omniscient. Believe in Him today! *"If you can believe, all things are possible to him who believes"* (Mark 9:23).

When we pray, we are admonished not to doubt. We must be specific in what we want God to do in us, through us and for us. James 1:6-7 says, *"But let him ask in faith, with no doubting, for he who doubts is like a wave of the sea driven and tossed by the wind. For let not that man suppose that he will receive anything from the Lord, he is a double-minded man, unstable in all his ways."*

An account is given of a man by the name of Stephen who was mightily used of God in the early church. Stephen was not a Pastor or an Evangelist. He was chosen to serve in the ushering/hospitality ministry. However, he believed in an extraordinary God and as a result of His faith in an extraordinary God, he did extraordinary things. *"And Stephen, full of faith and power, did great wonders and signs among the people" (Acts 6:8)*.

The Word of God is full of illustrations of people who found themselves in all manner of predicaments and crisis, but through faith in God they emerged triumphantly. *"And what more shall I say?*

For the time would fail me to tell of Gideon and Barak and Samson and Jephthah also of David and Samuel and the prophets who through faith subdued kingdoms, worked righteousness, obtained promises, stopped the mouth of lions, quenched the violence of fire, escaped the edge of the sword, out of weakness were made strong, became valiant in battle, turned to fight the armies of aliens. Women received their dead raised to life again" (Hebrews 11:32-35).

We overcome setbacks, challenges and attacks of the enemy through faith in God. *"For whatever is born of God overcomes the world. And this is the victory that has overcome the world, our faith" (1 John 5:4).*

Chapter 7

The Secret Weapon of Fasting

Fasting crucifies our flesh and brings us closer to God. Fasting adds fuel to our prayers. Some conditions, hardships, strongholds, bondages and oppressions of the enemy require fasting for the power of the enemy to be broken. In **Mark 9,** the disciples were unable to deliver a boy from a deaf and dumb spirit. The boy's father brought him to Jesus. Jesus rebuked the unclean spirit from the boy and immediately he was set free and healed. When the disciples asked Jesus why they could not cast out the spirit out of this boy, Jesus replied, *"this kind can come out by nothing but prayer and fasting" (Mark 9:29).*

Jesus told His disciples in **Matthew 6:16-19,** *"Moreover, when you fast, do not be like the hypocrites, with a sad countenance. For they disfigure their faces that they may appear to men to be fasting. Assuredly I say to you, they have their reward. But you when you fast, anoint your head and wash your face, so that you do not appear to men to be fasting, but to your Father who is in the secret place and your father who sees in secret will reward you openly."*

Jesus was admonishing His disciples that they did not have to let the whole world know they were fasting by appearing miserable and weak! There is a reward for fasting. Whatever you are interceding for, added with fasting, will release the power of God in your situation mightily. The God, who sees your sincerity and hears your prayer, will intervene on your behalf. You do not have to announce to everyone that you are fasting because your Heavenly Father who sees in secret will reward you openly.

The early church prayed concerning everything and fasted frequently. They prayed and fasted before they ministered, *"As they ministered to the Lord and fasted, the Holy Spirit said, now separate to me Barnabas and Saul for the work to which I have called them. Then having fasted and prayed and laid hands on them, they sent them away" (Acts 13:2-3).*

They prayed and fasted concerning selection of church leaders, *"So when they had appointed elders in every church and prayed with fasting, they commanded them to the Lord in whom they had believed" (Acts 14:23).*

The Book of Esther describes Esther's remarkable rise to power because of the favor of God upon her life. Yet there was a point in her life when she could no longer rely on her beauty, her status or the fact that she was a queen to get the hand of God to move on her behalf. Her predicament was so severe she needed to add fasting to her prayers. Her native people were about to be annihilated through a very well devised wicked scheme. Queen Esther knew she needed the supernatural intervention of the Almighty God to save them. So she resorted to prayer and fasting and the results were outstanding! *"Go gather all the Jews who are present in Shushan and fast for me, neither eat nor drink for three days, night or day. My maids and I will fast likewise"* **(Esther 4:16).**

The power of fasting, first of all, gave Esther favor and access to the king even though he had not officially summoned her. She was able to share with the king the plight of the Jewish people. The power of fasting caused Haman, who had devised the wicked plot against the Jews, to be exposed and he ended up hanging on the very gallows he had prepared for Mordecai, Queen Esther's

Uncle. *"So they hanged Haman on the gallows that he had prepared for Mordecai" (Esther 7:10).*

The Great King Jehosophat reached a time in his life when his well trained army could not help him or his famous reputation. He was surrounded by a multitude of enemy armies and needed the power of God to deliver him from the onslaught of them. What did he do? He called a fast. *"And Jehosophat feared and set himself to seek the Lord and proclaimed a fast throughout all Judah" (2 Chronicles 20:3).*

As they sought the Lord in fasting, a prophetic word came forth that gave them direction and strategy on how to defeat the enemy. The results of their fasting were beyond anything they had expected! Not only were their enemies defeated, there was so much spoil that it took three days to carry away the spoils of war*! "When Jehosophat and his people came to take away their spoil, they found among them an abundance of valuables among the dead bodies and precious jewels which they stripped off for themselves ,more than they could carry away and they were three days gathering the spoil because there was so much" (2 Chronicles 20:25).*

Nineveh was scheduled for God's judgment due to sin and wickedness being prevalent in the land. But they humbled themselves before God in prayer by repenting and fasting and God showed mercy upon them. *"So the people of Nineveh believed God, proclaimed a fast, and put on sackcloth, from the greatest to the least of them. Then word came to the king of Nineveh and he arose from his throne and laid aside his robe, covered himself with sackcloth and sat in ashes. And he caused it to be proclaimed and published throughout Nineveh by the decree of the king and his nobles saying, let neither man nor beast, herd nor flock, taste anything, do not let them eat, or drink water. But let man and beast be covered with sackcloth and cry mightily to God, yes let every one turn from his evil way and from the violence that is in his hands. Who can tell if God will turn and relent and turn away from His fierce anger, so that we may not perish? Then God saw their works that they turned from their evil way and God relented from the disaster that he had said He would bring upon them and He did not do it"* *(Jonah 3:5-10).*

What are you battling with today, child of God? What issue have you been struggling with for years? What do you need God to do for you in this season? Maybe you have tried in your own strength and power, but your efforts have come to naught. Is it your wayward teenage children? Is it marital problems? Is it unending financial distress? Call on the Lord in prayer and fasting. The Lord will hear your cry. As we saw from the above illustrations, God is so faithful to intervene when His people call out to Him in prayer and fasting. *"Hear me when I call, O God of my righteousness! You have relieved me in my distress, have mercy on me and hear my prayer" (Psalms 4:1).*

Fasting destroys the strongholds of the enemy. Fasting destroys all manner of addictions, bondages and oppressions. Anything that has kept you prisoner for years, fasting can destroy. Fasting brings about great deliverance. When Daniel was thrown into a den of lions, it was the secret weapon of fasting on his behalf that supernaturally delivered him.

"Now The King went to his palace and spent the night fasting and no musicians were brought before him. And his sleep went from him. Then the King arose very early in the morning and went in haste to the den of lions. And when he came to the den, he cried out with a lamenting voice to Daniel. The King spoke saying to Daniel, Daniel servant of the Living God, has your God whom you serve continually been able to deliver you from the lions. Then Daniel said to the King, O King live forever. My God sent His angel and shut the lions mouths so that they have not hurt me, because I was found innocent before Him and also O King I have done no wrong before you" (Daniel 6:18-22).

Daniel's supernatural deliverance so impacted King Darius that he made a decree acknowledging that the God of Daniel was the Living God. *"I make a decree that in every dominion of my kingdom men must tremble and fear before the God of Daniel, for He is the Living God and steadfast forever. His Kingdom is the one which shall not be destroyed and His dominion shall endure to the end. He delivers and rescues and He works signs and wonders in heaven and on earth, who has delivered Daniel from the power of the lions" (Daniel 6:26-27).*

When Nehemiah heard that the wall of Jerusalem had been broken down, he was so distraught that he cried out to the Lord in prayer and fasting. *"So it was when I heard those words, that I sat down and wept and mourned for many days. I was fasting and praying before the God of heaven" (Nehemiah 1:4).* Nehemiah repented on behalf of the people of Judah because it was due to their sin that they had been scattered as a people, captured by their enemies and their wall broken down. Nehemiah prayed in humility and sincerity, asking God to forgive their sins. He went on to pray that God might grant him favor before the King so that he could return to his homeland to rebuild what the enemy had destroyed. God gave him favor with the King, and Nehemiah was released to go and restore and rebuild the broken wall of the temple in Jerusalem. He successfully rebuilt the temple in one year.

Chapter 8

Mixing Your Prayers With Giving

Throughout the Word of God, we read stories of men and women who touched the heart of God through their giving. We are familiar with Abraham who waited for twenty-five years for a son. Just as Abraham was enjoying his long awaited son, Isaac -- *"Now it came to pass after these things that God tested Abraham and said to him, Abraham. And he said, here I am. Then He said, Take now your only son Isaac whom you love and go to the land of Moriah and offer him there as a burnt offering on one of the mountains which I shall tell you" (Genesis 22:1-2).*

We can only imagine what Abraham must have felt hearing those words from the Almighty God. He and his wife, Sarah, had waited for twenty-five years for this miracle child. They were old. Maybe if they were young, they could have easily and readily given him up, knowing that they could have another child. Their son was their prized possession, the apple of their eyes, and they had even named him, Isaac, meaning, "laughter". Abraham had obeyed God in all other matters, but this would be the ultimate test.

Despite how he was feeling and not understanding this request, Abraham proceeded to obey God. *"Then they came to the place of which God had told him. And Abraham built an altar there and place the wood in order and he bound Isaac his son and laid him on the altar, upon the wood. And Abraham stretched out his hand and took the knife to slay his son. But the angel of the Lord called to him from heaven and said, Abraham, Abraham! So he said, here I am. And He said, Do not lay your hand on the lad or do anything to him, for now I know that you fear God, since you have not withheld your son, your only son from me"* *(Genesis 22:9-12).*

I am always challenged by Abraham's obedience and willingness to give the Lord what he loved the most. His willingness to obey God caused him to walk in unprecedented blessing. *"Then the angel of the Lord called to Abraham a second time out of heaven and said, By Myself I have sworn, says the Lord because you have done this thing and have not withheld, your son, your only son, blessing I will bless you and multiplying I will multiply your descendants as the stars of heaven and as the sand which is on the seashore and our descendants shall possess the gate of their enemies. In your seed, all the nations of the earth shall be blessed, because you have obeyed My voice"* *(Genesis 22:15-18).*

Abraham was blessed beyond measure. In addition to being a man of prayer and faith, he understood the principle of sacrificial giving. The blessing of the Lord in his life went as far as the next generation. His son, Isaac, was blessed. His grandsons Jacob and Esau were blessed. And his great-grandson, Joseph, was so mightily blessed that he became the Prime Minister in a foreign land! This is how powerful our sacrificial giving and willingness to obey can be.

Hannah was desperate for a child. Even though her husband Elkanah loved and cherished her, it was not enough. To make matters worse, her co-wife, Peninah, tormented, provoked and mistreated her. In our generation, having children is not a big deal. Many couples are even opting not to have children. Those who desire children, but are unable to have children naturally have medical technology to thank as there are now numerous options and alternatives available for couples who are having trouble conceiving. However, in biblical times, having children was of utmost importance. To be married and not have children was a shameful thing. Marriage without children was considered not a marriage. In those days, families had a lot of land and property and one of the primary reasons for having all this land and property was for the children to help their parents till the land. In addition, when parents passed away, the land could remain in the family and be passed on to the children, the next generation.

It is with this background that we can understand Hannah's predicament, torment and pain of being childless. She felt unworthy as a wife, disrespected and looked down upon by society. There were no medical alternatives or technologies she could turn to. After praying for many years for a child, with no results, she decided to take her prayer to another level; she mixed her prayers with sacrificial giving. *"Then she made a vow and said, O Lord of hosts, if you will indeed look on the affliction of your maidservant and remember me and not forget your maidservant, but will give your maidservant a male child, then I will give him to the Lord all the days of your life and no razor shall come upon her head" (I Samuel 2:11).*

Hannah's vow provoked God and she miraculously conceived after they returned home. **"And Elkanah knew his wife and the Lord remembered her.** *So it came to pass in the process of time that Hannah conceived and bore a son, and called his name, Samuel, saying, because I have asked for him from the Lord"* (*1 Samuel 2:19-20).* After she weaned him, she brought him to the Temple in obedience to her vow. *"Now when she had weaned him, she took him up with her, with three bulls, one ephah of flour, and a skin of wine, and brought him to the house of the Lord in Shiloh. For this child I prayed and the Lord has granted me my petition which I asked of Him. Therefore I also have lent him to the Lord, as long as He lives he shall be lent to the Lord"* (*I Samuel 1:24, 27-28).*

God honored her obedience by blessing her with more children. *"And the Lord visited Hannah so that she conceived and bore three sons and two daughters. Meanwhile the child Samuel grew before the Lord"* (*I Samuel 2: 21).* We can never out give God. He honors our sacrificial giving. Whenever He requires us to give, we obey knowing beyond a shadow of a doubt, He has a huge blessing in store for those who are willing and obedient.

Hannah's miracle son, Samuel, was no ordinary child. He was called, chosen and anointed of God as a prophet while he was still in his mother's womb. Samuel grew to be a prophet of God. One who feared God and became God's mouthpiece to the people. *"So Samuel grew and the Lord was with him and let none of his words fall to the ground" (1 Samuel 3:19).* A time came when Israel was badly defeated by the Philistines due to their sin and whoring after other gods. The children of Israel came to The Prophet Samuel for help and said, *"Do not cease to cry out to the Lord our God for us, that He may save us from the hand of the Philistines. And Samuel took a suckling lamb and offered it as a whole burnt offering to the Lord. Then Samuel cried out to the Lord for Israel and the Lord answered him. Now as Samuel was offering up the burnt offering, the Philistines drew near to battle against Israel. But the Lord thundered with a loud thunder upon the Philistines that day and so confused them that they were overcome before Israel. So the Philistines were subdued and they did not come anymore into the territory of Israel. And the hand of the Lord was against the Philistines all the days of Samuel. Then the cities which the Philistines had taken from Israel were restored to Israel" (1 Samuel 7:8-10, 13-14).*

Not only did God answer the Israelites through the prayers and giving of the Prophet Samuel, but during Samuel's lifetime the Philistines did not make war with him and the land. Everything was restored that the

Philistines took from Israel! I cannot overemphasize the power of sacrificial giving to the Lord. Our sacrificial giving steers Him to action on our behalf! Our sacrificial giving opens the windows of heaven. He always does more than we can imagine!

Before the Prophet Samuel died, he anointed a young shepherd boy called David to be the second King of Israel. David was a great King, a worshipper of God, a mighty man of war, a skilled warrior, and an intercessor for God's people. However, David was not perfect. When he sinned, he was quick to repent and David also knew how important it was to mix his prayers with sacrificial giving to the Lord.

"Now Satan stood up against Israel and moved David to number Israel. And God was displeased with this thing, therefore he struck Israel. So David said to God, I have sinned greatly because I have done this thing, but now I pray take away the iniquity of your Servant, for I have done very foolishly. Then David said to Ornan, grant me the place of this threshing floor, that I may build an altar on it to the Lord. You shall grant it to me at the full price that the plague may be withdrawn from the people. Then King David said to Ornan, No but I will surely buy it for the full price, for I will not take what is yours for the Lord, nor offer burnt offerings with that which costs me nothing. So David gave Ornan six

hundred shekels of gold by weight for the place. And David built there an altar to the Lord and offered burnt offerings and peace offerings and called on the Lord and he answered him from heaven by fire on the altar of burnt offering" (1 Chronicles 21:1, 7-8, 22, 2426.) Ornan was willing to give the threshing floor freely to David, but David refused to receive it in this manner. As soon as he sacrificed to the Lord, God answered him by fire and the plague immediately stopped.

David had a son called Solomon who reigned after him. At the beginning of Solomon's reign, he spent time in prayer in the presence of the Lord. *"And Solomon went up there to the bronze altar before the Lord, which was at the tabernacle of meeting and offered a thousand burnt offerings on it. On that night God appeared to Solomon and said to him, Ask what shall I give you? Now give me wisdom and knowledge that I may go out and come in before this people, for who can judge this great people of yours. Then God said to Solomon, because this was in your heart and you have not asked riches or wealth or honor or the life of your enemies, nor have you asked long life, but have asked wisdom and knowledge for yourself that you may judge my people over whom I made you king, wisdom and knowledge are granted to you and I will give you riches and wealth and honor, such as none of the*

Kings have had who were before you, nor shall any after you have the like" *(2 Chronicles 1:6-7, 10-11).*

Solomon's prayer was simple. He needed wisdom to rule and guide the nation of Israel. But before he made his request, he gave a generous offering to the Lord of a thousand lambs. God not only granted him his request for wisdom, but in addition, gave him great wealth, honor, majesty and splendor that he had not requested. God gave Solomon such wisdom that people traveled from thousands of miles to come and hear his wisdom. ***"So King Solomon surpassed all the kings of the earth in riches and wisdom. Now all the earth sought the presence of Solomon to hear his wisdom, which God had put in his heart"*** *(1 Kings 10:23-24).*

God gave Solomon such wealth and honor that when the Queen of Sheba, who was very wealthy in her own right, saw all his wealth, she fainted! ***"And when The Queen of Sheba had seen the wisdom of Solomon, the house that he built, the food on his table, the seating of his servants, the service of his waiters and their apparel, and his entry way by which he went up to the house of the Lord, there was no more spirit in her"*** *(2 Chronicles 9:3).*

I want to encourage you in this season to honor the Lord with your sacrificial giving. Take your prayer life to another level by giving sacrificially, especially if you have been in a crisis for an unusual length of time. Be a faithful and consistent tither in your local church and a generous giver of offerings to advance the Kingdom of God. Do not give God your leftovers. Do not give Him that which does not cost you anything because your giving is a memorial to God. Cornelius was visited by an angel because his prayers and giving had become a memorial in heaven! *"There was a certain man in Caesarea called Cornelius, a centurion, a devout man and one who feared God with all his household who gave alms generously to the people and prayed to God always. About the ninth hour of the day, he saw clearly in a vision, an angel of God coming in and saying to him, Cornelius! And when he observed him, he was afraid, and said, what is it Lord, the angel said, Your prayers and your alms have come up for a memorial before God" (Acts 10:1-4).*

The early church in the Book of Acts was not only a praying church, but a giving church. They were so blessed financially that none in their midst had a need! *"Nor was there anyone among them who lacked, for all who were possessors of landsor houses sold them and brought the proceeds of the things that were sold and laid them at the apostles feet, and they*

distributed to each one as anyone had need" *(Acts 4: 34-35).*

The Apostle Paul when he wrote to the Church at Philippi, he thanked the Church for their prayers and their financial support of his ministry. *"I thank my God upon every remembrance of you, always in every prayer of mine making request for you all with joy, for your fellowship (partnership) in the gospel from the first day until now"* *(Philippians 1:3-5).*

Change your life, family, destiny and ministry by sacrificially giving to The Lord. Provoke God with an unusual gift this season and get ready for the door you have been desiring to be opened, to be open. Get ready for the Lord to do exceedingly and abundantly above all you can ask or think in every area of your life.

Chapter 9

Contending For Your Prophetic Purpose & Destiny

Each one of us has a divine assignment to fulfill on the earth. God has glorious plan for each of our lives. The enemy also has a plan for us and it is to abort the vision and dream God has for His people. The Apostle Paul told his spiritual son, Timothy, *"This charge I commit to you, son Timothy according to the prophecies previously made concerning you, that by them you may wage the good warfare" (1 Timothy 1:18).* Paul was letting Timothy know that he would have to pray through the prophecies concerning his life. He could not afford to sit back, relax and "wait" for the prophecies to come to pass. He had to war in prayer.

We must not and cannot rest until the promises of God become a reality in our lives. Let us refuse to be content with second best and let us refuse the devil's handouts and leftovers. We have an inheritance in Jesus Christ! We are heirs of God and joint heirs with Jesus Christ. We are called to walk in the fullness of our calling and bring transformation to the earth. This will never happen if we don't pray! **Isaiah 62:1, 6-7 says,** *For Zion's sake, I will not hold my peace, and for Jerusalem's sake I will not rest, until her righteousness goes forth as brightness, and her salvation as a lamp that burns. I have set watchmen on your walls, Oh Jerusalem, they shall never hold their peace day or night, you who make mention of the Lord, do not keep silent, and give Him no rest until He establishes, And till he makes Jerusalem a praise in the earth."*

God is giving us a right to bombard Him until the answer is released! He says, **"You who make mention of The Lord do NOT keep silent!"** In other words, keep praying until your dream comes to fruition and your vision is realized. God is giving us express permission to give Him **no rest "until He establishes and until He makes Jerusalem a praise in the earth"** Your "Jerusalem" could be your marriage, family, children, business, church, ministry or education. Whatever your Jerusalem is, do not give up praying until it becomes what God said it would become . . . glorious and breathtaking to behold !

Isaiah 43:26 declares, **"Put Me in remembrance, let us contend together, state your case that you may be acquitted."** Again, the Lord is telling His people to remind Him of your situation, your issue, and your concerns. He also uses legal terminology, *"state your case that you may be acquitted."* In a court of law you submit evidence. The Lord is telling us to submit evidence concerning our various situations in the heavenly court of law that we may be acquitted.

God wants to hear from you! What are you going through? What are you believing God for? What dream are you carrying that has not come to pass? Do not keep it to yourself tell the Lord your God! You were not created for mediocrity and complacency. You were created to make an impact in your generation. Your presence must be felt. You must leave a legacy. That is why it is imperative that you pray for the Lord to reveal your divine assignment upon the earth. *"Present your case, says the Lord, bring forth your strong reasons, says the King of Jacob" (Isaiah 41:21).*

I marvel at the authority and access our God has given us to receive from Him. He says in *Isaiah 45:11, "Ask Me of things to come concerning My sons, and concerning the work of My hands, you command me.*" In other words, He is giving us the authority and permission not only to ask about the future, but also to place a demand on Him and command Him concerning our desires, petitions, and requests! Every believer is an Ambassador of Jesus Christ, and as Ambassadors, we represent the Kingdom of heaven, upon the earth. Through prayer, we become spiritual law enforcement agents of God, destroying powers of darkness and enforcing the Word of God and His purposes and plans upon the earth.

Friend, this scripture should inspire and provoke you to pray! In the same manner that biological children ask their parents their future plans and place demands for certain things, our Heavenly Father has given us this same right! Let us not remain spiritually passive, complacent and lethargic. Let us arise in fervent and effective prayer. Let us contend for our prophetic purpose and destiny. Let us be persistent like the psalmist David, who said, *"As for me I will call upon God, and the Lord shall save me, evening and morning and at noon, I will pray and cry aloud and He shall hear my voice. He has redeemed my soul in peace from the battle that was against me" (Psalms 55:16-18).*

The enemy will not sit idly by as you fulfill your destiny. He will do everything in his limited power to oppose, discourage and frustrate you as a child of God. **Remember satan's power and knowledge is limited. Our God is All powerful and All knowing.** That is why we have to arise with holy anger and righteous indignation. We have to get spiritually angry at Christian marriages that are being plagued with separation and divorce. We have to arise against spiritual laziness and prayerlessness in our own lives and in the Body of Christ. We have to refuse every package of the enemy. *"And from the days of John the Baptist until now, the Kingdom of heaven suffers violence and the violent take it by force" (Matthew 11:12).* We have to violently in prayer and in the spirit take our families, finances, communities, cities and nations back from the grip of Satan and back to God.

In fact, God is looking upon the earth for someone He can use to bring healing, restoration and transformation through the power of prayer. *"The Lord looks down from heaven upon the children of men, to see if there are any who understand who seek God" (Psalms 14:2).*

This is the hour to contend for your destiny: your family's destiny, your ministry's destiny, your business's destiny, and for your finances' destiny. This is the season to go after God and pursue Him with all your strength and might. This is the time to see your vision come to pass and your dream a reality. You may be facing delays in your life, and all hell seems to be breaking loose and your situation is completely opposite to the promise. **Psalms 50:15** declares, however, *"Call Upon me in the day of trouble, I will deliver you and you will glorify me."*

Refuse to give up and refuse to give in until all that God spoke concerning your life, your marriage, your family, your finances, your career, and your ministry comes to pass. There is so much we have not yet experienced. God has so much in store for us. We will only apprehend our inheritance through prayer. **Jeremiah 33:3 says, "Call to me and I will answer you, and show you great and mighty things which you do not know"**

The apostles knew they could only fulfill the call of God on their lives only through consistent, fervent prayer. When a dispute arose in the early church concerning a section of widows who were not being served, the apostles made a wise decision. , and that is to delegate this responsibility as they remain in prayer and meditating on The Word of God. *"Then the twelve summoned the multitude of the disciples and said, It is not desirable that we should leave the word of God and serve tables, therefore brethren, seek out from among you seven men of good reputation, full of the Holy Spirit and wisdom, whom we may appoint over this business, but we will give ourselves continually to prayer and the ministry of the Word" (Acts 6:2-4).* To operate in the anointing that they flowed in, they had to continually be in His presence in prayer and in the Word of God. They had to saturate themselves in prayer and in the scriptures.

I believe by now we have seen that prayer is not just aimless, half-hearted chatter whereby empty words are mumbled. Child of God, you have been given power! Jesus told His disciples, *"Behold I give you the authority to trample on serpents and scorpions and over all the power of the enemy and nothing shall by any means hurt you" (Luke 10:19).* Effective Prayer must be strategic. In order to fulfill your destiny, you must be focused (determined, persistent and persuaded). Hold on to the promise of God concerning your future and destiny. When you pray sincerely, specifically, on target through the power of the Holy Spirit, believing God against all odds, the mountains and challenges that seemed so insurmountable and impossible become small and insignificant compared to the greatness of God.

The Word of God is full of scriptures that reveal our identity in God, the great plan He has for our lives, and His great desire to answer our prayers. *"And do not seek what you should eat or what you should drink, nor have an anxious mind, for all these things the nations of the world seek after and your Father knows that you need these things. But seek the kingdom of God and all these things shall be added to you. Do not fear little flock for it is your father's good pleasure to give you the Kingdom" (Luke 12:29-32).*

The disciples of Jesus saw first hand the effect and impact Jesus' ministry had wherever they went. The Word of God was taught in power and authority, demons were being cast out of people, the sick were being miraculously healed, and those that were bound and oppressed were supernaturally delivered by the power of God. They asked Jesus to teach them how to pray because they knew the secret to His success was prayer. *"Now it came to pass, as He was praying in a certain place, when he ceased, that one of his disciples said to Him Lord, teach us to pray as John also taught his disciples. So He said to them, When you pray say, Our Father is heaven, hallowed be thy name your kingdom come, your will be done, on earth as it is in heaven, give us day by day our daily bread and forgive us our sins, for we also forgive everyone who is indebted to us and do not lead us into temptation, but deliver us from evil" (Luke 11:1-4).*

The key aspect of this prayer is, *"your kingdom come your will be done on earth as it is in heaven."* We pray for God's Kingdom to infiltrate and cover the earth. His Kingdom releases power, authority, dominion, order, righteousness, joy, peace, victory, salvation, deliverance, healing, protection, provision, unity, and purpose. Pray "they kingdom come" in your marriage, family, home, work, business, ministry, church, neighborhhood, city and nation .

You were not created to lead a dull, boring and monotonous life. You were created by the Almighty God to do exploits - *"Those who know their God shall be strong and do exploits" (Daniel 11:32).* In prayer we get to know God, His nature, His power, His ability, His love, His mercy, His steadfastness, His greatness, His sovereignty, His majesty and His glory. When you get a glimpse of Him, faith rises in you because you come to the realization of how gloriously awesome He is. His power that is released when we pray enable us to achieve the extraordinary, the impossible and the unusual.

We become intimate with God as we spend time in His presence studying His Word and praying. Through His infallible, unchanging Word, we get to know His character. He is all powerful, all knowing, all seeing, and more than able to sustain us. He is faithful. He is good. He is merciful. Let prayer become a lifestyle. *"But I give myself to prayer" (Psalms 109:4b).*

We were created to make an impact in our generation. We were created to be history makers, trailblazers and world changers. We are the **light of the world** and the **salt of the earth.** Wherever we go, we should bring transformation. God chose us before the foundation of the world to do great things on the earth on His behalf. We are called to touch our generation and leave a legacy that can be passed onto future generations. Through prayer, we discover our purpose and destiny in Christ. *"For we are His workmanship, created in Christ Jesus for good works which God prepared beforehand that we should walk in them" (Ephesians 2:10).*

Child of God, I want to encourage you not to give up on your dream or destiny. Yes, it has been a long journey. Yes, you have had to go through many trials and tribulations. Yes, there have been setbacks and challenges, but you have come this far by faith. You cannot give up now! There is a light at the end of the tunnel. It's your season to rejoice. You have cried for this too long. Wipe away those tears. Pick yourself up and be encouraged in the Lord -- *"Weeping may endure for a night, but joy comes in the morning" (Psalms 30:5b).* Be encouraged in the Lord. You will be strengthened in His presence as you wait upon Him.

"Have you not known? Have you not heard? The everlasting God, the Lord, the Creator of the ends of the earth, neither faints nor is weary. His understanding is unsearchable. He gives power to the weak, and to those who have

no might he increases strength. Even the youths shall faint and be weary, and the young men shall utterly fail, but those who wait upon the Lord shall renew their strength, they shall mount up with wings as eagles, they shall run and not be weary, they shall walk and not faint" (Isaiah 40:28-31).

As you contend for your destiny, pray with the revelation that the Lord your God is a Man of War. *"Who is this King of glory, the Lord strong and mighty, the Lord mighty in battle" (Psalms 24:8).* From Genesis to Revelation, our God is a Man of War; He has never lost a battle.

As you pray, the enemy hears the voice of the Lord through you. *"The voice of the Lord is over the waters, the God of glory thunders, the Lord is over many waters, the voice of the Lord is powerful, the voice of the Lord is full of majesty" (Psalms 29:3-4).*

Daniel contended not only for his own destiny, but for the destiny of the Jewish people. Jeremiah prophesied that the Jewish people would be in captivity in Babylon for 70 years. However, the 70 years had passed and the Jewish people were still in captivity. This disturbed Daniel's spirit, so he began to seek the Lord in prayer and fasting, repenting on behalf of the people and reminding God of His promise to deliver them from captivity.

Then angel of the Lord appeared unto Daniel and told him the future of the Jewish people.

"Then he said to me, Do not fear Daniel for from the first day that you set your heart to understand and to humble yourself before your God, your words were heard and I have come because of your words. But the prince of the kingdom of Persia withstood me twenty one days and behold Michael, one of the Chief Princes came to help me" (Daniel 10:12-13).

Daniel had to contend for his destiny and for the destiny of his people. As soon as he began to pray, a demonic spirit tried to block his prayers. Daniel's persistence in prayer and fasting broke the demonic influence of delay and denial and the angel of the Lord was able to deliver the message. I challenge you to arise and pray for your destiny, for your future, and for your family. The prophetic promise you are carrying needs to be "prayed through."

Let us refuse to back down. Let us refuse to be denied our rightful inheritance. Let us refuse to settle for second best. Let us refuse to live a mediocre and average life. In addition to Daniel, there are so many examples in the Word of God of ordinary people who did extraordinary things because they dared to go all the way with God. They dared to believe God despite their natural circumstances. They contended for their prophetic purpose and destiny with resilience and determination. *"Therefore we also, since we are surrounded by so great a cloud of witnesses, let us lay aside every weight, and the sin which so easily ensnares us and let us run with endurance the race that is set before us, looking unto Jesus, the author and finisher of our faith, who for the joy that was set before Him endured the cross, despising the shame, and has sat down at the right hand of the throne of God" (Hebrews 12:1-2).*

The Lord desires to complete the good work He started in you. When He starts a work, He completes it. He does not leave you halfway. He did not bring you this far to leave you. He is a God of performance. *"I will cry out to God Most High; to God who performs all things for me" (Psalms 57:2).*

Ultimately, all power and might belong to our God. He is the Omnipotent and Omniscient God. He is the Creator of the universe. Satan and all his demons cannot even compare in power and might; they are only creations. Our God is the Creator and He reigns supreme in glory and majesty. *"The Lord reigns, let the earth rejoice, let the multitude of isles be glad, clouds and darkness surround Him, Righteousness and justice are the foundation of His throne, A fire goes before Him and burns up all His enemies round about, the earth sees and trembles. The mountains melt*

like wax at the presence of the Lord" **(Psalms 97:1-5).**

We have no excuse not to pray, as we make time for so many other things in our lives, let us make time for The Lord, it is worth it ! Beloved, pray with expectancy, pray with joy, pray with anticipation because the time you are spending in His glorious presence shall yield results, as the scripture puts it, " . . **Eye has not seen, nor ear heard, nor have entered into the heart of man, the things which God has prepared for those who love him."** 1 Corinthians 2:9

Prophetic Word of Encouragement

As I began working on this book, my spirit was excited. I knew it was God's timing because the Holy Spirit was stirring me to write. There were so many distractions, setbacks and challenges, but through the power of the Holy Spirit I have prevailed and the Lord has enabled me to complete this book. I have had to literally pray through and persevere to complete this book. Prayer works! I have had to live out what I am sharing with you.

As I conclude, my spirit within me is leaping for joy as I know that I know that I know that the God of breakthrough also known as Jehovah Balperazim is about to visit someone's life, family, home, school, business, ministry *and* church. When God visits you, you never remain the same! When God visits you, those around recognize the change! His visitation is tangible. Are you ready for God's visitation *?*

it is time for you to testify of the goodness of The Lord, it is time for you to sing the song, 'look what The Lord has done' It is time to rejoice because of the supernatural intervention of God in your affairs! **"The voice of rejoicing and salvation is in the tents of the righteous, the right hand of the Lord does valiantly, the right hand of the Lord is exalted . . ." (Psalms 118:15-16).**

When you decide to pursue the Lord, regardless of the price you have to pay, but you make up your mind to touch the heart of God through prayer, there will be breakthroughs in your life and everything concerning you. People around you will say, *"This was the Lord's doing. It is marvelous in our eyes. This is the day the Lord has made, we will rejoice and be glad in it" (Psalms 118:23-24)* - purpose in your heart that this year will be a special year for you. You cannot keep struggling with the same issues. You cannot remain the same. You must persevere in prayer, knowing that, *"The Lord is near to all who call upon Him, to all who call upon Him in truth. He will fulfill the desire of those who fear Him. He will also hear their cry and save them" (Psalms 145:18-19).*

Isn't it about time you begin living your dream? Isn't it about time your vision come to pass? Child of God, be of good cheer. There shall be a demonstration of the power of God in your life. There shall be a manifestation of the glory of God in your life. There shall be a fulfillment of the promises of God in your life. When an angel visited Mary and told her she would carry the promised Messiah, in the natural it did not make sense, but she believed anyway. The Holy Spirit spoke through her cousin, Elizabeth, and said, *"Blessed is she who believed, for there will be a fulfillment of those things*

which were told her from the Lord" (Luke 1:45).

Pray in the Spirit. Pray standing on the Word of God. Have faith in God as you pray. Utilize the weapons of warfare that God has given you. Use your secret weapon of fasting. Mix your prayers with sacrificial giving and watch God completely transform your life!

Expect supernatural intervention in your affairs. Expect God to do the unbelievable and impossible. I pray you have been stirred to pray like never before. If you are an intercessor already, I pray this book will ignite and propel you to a higher dimension of prayer.

It's your time, it's your season ! You are unstoppable, unbeatable, unshakeable and unmoveable in The Name of Jesus Christ, Son of The Living God !

Chapter 10

Scriptures on Prayer

Throughout the Bible there are various references to men and women who called upon the Lord and He answered them. Here are a few examples that you can use not only for yourself when you are in need, but to stand in the gap for others.

"Now therefore, restore the man's wife, for he is a prophet and he will pray for you and you shall live . . . So Abraham prayed to God and God healed Abimelech, his wife and his female servants. Then they bore children" (Genesis 20:7, 17).

"Then Jacob was left alone and a Man wrestled with him until the breaking of

day. Now when He saw that He did not prevail against Him, He touched the socket of his hip and the socket of Jacob's hip was out of joint as He wrestled with him and He said, let me go for the day breaks, But he said, I will not let you go unless you bless me" (Genesis 32:24-26).

"Then the children of Israel groaned because of the bondage and they cried out and their cry came up to God because of the bondage. So God heard their groaning and God remembered His covenant with Abraham, with Isaac and with Jacob. And God looked upon the children of Israel and God acknowledged them" (Exodus 2:23-25).

"Then Joshua spoke to the Lord in the day when the Lord delivered up the Amorites before the children of Israel, and he said in the sight of Israel, Sun stand still over Gibeon and Moon in the Valley of Aijalon, so the sun stood still and the moon stopped, till the people had revenge, upon their enemies, is this not written in the book of Jasher? So the sun stood still in the midst of heaven and did not hasten to go down for about a whole day, And there has been no day like that, before it or after it, that the Lord heeded a voice of a man, for the Lord fought for Israel" (Joshua 10:12-14).

"And she was in bitterness of soul, and prayed to the Lord and wept in anguish. Then Eli answered and said, Go in peace and the God of Israel grant your petition which you have asked of him. And Elkannah knew Hannah his wife and the Lord remembered her" (1 Samuel 1:10, 18, 19).

"Continue earnestly in prayer, being vigilant in it with thanksgiving" (Colossians 4:2).

"Is anyone among you suffering? Let him pray. Is anyone among you sick? Let him call for the elders of the church, and let them pray over him, anointing him with oil in the name of the Lord. And the prayer of faith will save the sick, and the Lord will raise him up. And if he has committed sins, he will be forgiven. Confess your trespasses to one another, and pray for one another, that you may be healed. The effective fervent prayer of a righteous man avails much" (James 5:13-16).

"But know that the Lord has set apart for Himself him who is godly, the Lord will hear when I call to Him" (Psalms 4:3).

"Give heed to the voice of my cry, My King and My God, For to you I will pray, my voice you shall hear in the morning O Lord, in the morning, I will direct it to you and I will look up" (Psalms 5:2-3).

"Depart from me all you workers of iniquity, for the Lord has heard the voice of my weeping, the Lord has heard my supplication, the Lord will receive my prayer, let all my enemies be ashamed and greatly troubled, let them turn back and be suddenly ashamed" *(Psalms 6:8-10).*

"I have set the Lord always before me, because He is at my right hand, I shall not be moved" *(Psalms 16:8).*

"Hear a just cause O Lord, attend to my cry, give ear to my prayer which is not from deceitful lips" *(Psalms 17:1).*

"I have called upon you, for you will hear me O God, Incline your ear to me and hear my speech" *(Psalms 17:6).*

"May He grant you according to your heart's desire and fulfill all your purpose" *(Psalms 20:4).*

"Blessed be the Lord, because He has heard the voice of my supplication" *(Psalms 28:6).*

"For this cause everyone who is godly shall pray to you" *(Psalms 32:6).*

"This poor man cried out and the Lord heard him, and saved him out of all his troubles" *(Psalms 34:6).*

"The eyes of the Lord are on the righteous and His ears are open to their cry" (Psalms 34:15).

"The righteous cry out and the Lord hears and delivers them out of all their troubles" (Psalms 34:17).

"Cast your burden on the Lord and He shall sustain you, He shall never permit the righteous to be moved" (Psalms 55:22).

"O God you are My God, early will I seek you, my soul thirsts for you, my flesh longs for you, in a dry and thirsty land, where there is no water, so I have looked for you in the sanctuary, to see your power and your glory" (Psalms 63:1-2).

About Prophetess Mwaka Twagirayesu

Prophetess Mwaka Twagirayesu is a dynamic preacher and prolific teacher of the Word of God. She is an international conference speaker, psalmist, revivalist, church planter, author, entrepreneur, and a woman of prayer who operates under a powerful prophetic mantle with the gifts of the Spirit in operation. Her prophetic ministry has brought healing, restoration and transformation to thousands around the world. Countless testimonies of physical healings, spiritual revival, financial and business breakthroughs, miracles, signs and wonders are the trademark of her ministry.

Her family upbringing developed a passion for nations within her as a young girl, a daughter to diplomats as she is originally from Zambia, but grew up in Kenya. She went to University in England and the USA, and then later married Apostle Darius Twagirayesu from Rwanda. Prophetess Mwaka is the Founder and C.E.O of Fresh Aroma International Ministries, an apostolic and prophetic ministry birthed by the Holy Spirit, with a global mandate to release God's fragrance through the preaching of the Word of God and demonstration of the power of God, whether it is in churches, conventions, crusades, conferences, cities, nations, or around the world.

Prophetess Mwaka is a Kingdom Ambassador, who travels extensively challenging the Body of Christ to come out of complacency and mediocrity and become the people of power, purpose and influence they were created to be. Her prophetic ministry is accurate, her zeal for God is contagious, and her love for people is evident as she ministers with power and authority, yet with the simplicity and compassion of the Lord Jesus Christ. In addition to her busy ministry schedule, she uses her education as an Attorney, decade long work experience as a Family Resource Social Worker, Mediator and Philanthropist to bring community, national and global transformation.

Prophetess Mwaka and Apostle Darius Twagirayesu are the proud parents of three miracle boys: Zachary, age 13; Trey, age 11; and Prince, age 7. They are the Founders and Senior Pastors of All Nations House of Prayer Church in Irving, TX, USA.

Contact Information

Fresh Aroma International Ministries
2108 Hurd Drive, Suite 100
Irving, TX 75038
USA

For more information about Fresh Aroma Ministries, upcoming conferences and events, visit our website at www.fresharomaministry.org

Email: info@fresharomaministry.org

Tel # 469 288 4004

ORDER YOUR AUTOGRAPHED COPY TODAY!

NAME_____

ADDRESS_____

CITY _____

ST ._____ ZIP_____

PHONE _____

EMAIL_____

How may copies_____

Mail & make payment to:

Fresh Aroma International Ministries
2108 Hurd Drive, Suite 100
Irving, TX 75038
USA
Add $2 for Shipping & Handling